CAMBRIDGE OCTOCENTENARY
800
1201 – 2001

Cambridge
Evening News

Cambridge

The Story of a City

CHRIS ELLIOTT

breedon books
PUBLISHING

First published in Great Britain in 2001 by
The Breedon Books Publishing Company Limited
Breedon House, 3 The Parker Centre, Derby, DE21 4SZ.

ISBN 1 85983 242 3

Printed and bound by Butler & Tanner Ltd, Frome, Somerset
Jacket printing by GreenShires Ltd, Leicester

Contents

To Sue

Foreword

MANY books have been written about Cambridge, some focusing on the city's long history, some on its architecture, and some on its famous university, which is nearly eight centuries old. This book, compiled for publication in the year when the city itself celebrates the 800th anniversary of receiving its first royal charter, brings together those themes in one story. It recounts Cambridge's origins as a pre-Roman settlement, examines how it fell into the hands of successive foreign invaders, and chronicles the birth of Cambridge University, as well as the city's pivotal role in the Civil War, the experiences of its inhabitants during World War One and Two, and its phenomenal growth into the computer capital of Europe. Eight hundred years is a long time, and it has not been possible to mention every twist and turn in Cambridge's colourful past, nor the names of all those who have played a role in shaping the city today. For any omissions or truncation, I apologise.

Thanks are due to the library staff and photographers of the *Cambridge Evening News*, to the custodians of the Cambridgeshire Collection, to Cambridge University and its colleges, to Cambridge City Council, to Cambridge's business community, and to the authors of previous books about the city, whose work has been an invaluable source of reference.

Chris Elliott
Cambridge
Summer 2001

From Earliest Times

CAMBRIDGE is not a big city. In fact, it is one of the smallest in the United Kingdom, with a population of only 110,000 or so – about half the size of Nottingham, and only a quarter that of Manchester. It is not one of England's oldest cities either. Although its origins as a settlement go back to Roman times, it has been a city officially for only half a century, achieving that status in 1951. There is no doubt, however, that Cambridge is one of the most remarkable, and one of the most beautiful places in Britain, indeed anywhere in the world – and thanks to the dazzling achievements of its ancient university, it is also one of the most famous.

People have lived in and around Cambridge since the Stone Age. Archaeologists have found axes dating back to the Old Stone Age, or Palaeolithic times – possibly more than 300,000 years old – on a site west of the existing city. They have also unearthed tools and other domestic artefacts from the New Stone Age, or Neolithic period (9,000-4,000 BC), the Bronze Age (3,000-2,000 BC) and the Iron Age (600-500 BC), when the discovery of smelting gave people the ability to produce iron-bladed weapons, and farming implements like ploughshares.

The early inhabitants of the area lived mainly in very small communities, occupying homesteads or tiny settlements on the higher, drier ground on either side of the Cam, the river that runs through the city. From the latter part of the Neolithic period, when agriculture began to spread, many may have earned a living growing crops or farming sheep.

It was only with the coming of the Romans, in AD 43, that a sizeable town began to take shape. Mindful of the fact that they were invaders, and would need to be on their guard against attack, the Romans were careful to establish their bases in locations that were not only easy to defend, but which gave them strategic

Small but beautiful – Cambridge today.

Clues to the past – archaeologists excavating a site in the city centre.

domination. Cambridge was just such a spot. It was close to Ermine Street, the major Roman route from London northwards to Lincoln and York, and it had a perfect site for a fort – a steeply-rising slope, now known as Castle Hill, which was a superb vantage point, and ideal for defending the river crossing. The Romans duly built a camp there, and constructed a road from Colchester to Godmanchester, crossing the River Cam near where Magdalene Bridge is today, and linking up with what is now Huntingdon Road.

The secure presence of the Roman camp led to the birth of a little town adjacent to it, a collection of small, timber-framed houses with wattle and daub walls and thatched roofs. The people who lived there were a mix of Romans and indigenous Britons, and to serve their needs, potters' kilns and metal-working sites were soon up and running, with agricultural supplies coming in from Arbury Camp Farm to the north.

Historians differ on what Cambridge was called at this time. Some believe its name was Camborico, or Camboritum. Others think it was called Durolipons, meaning 'fortified place with a bridge'. Whatever its name, by the beginning of the fifth century AD the town had emerged as the urban centre for the surrounding area. People came there to buy goods, to trade, and to work, and it was an important inland port too. As well as building roads between big settlements, the Romans created a canal system in the Fens, with Cambridge as the most southerly navigable point. The town's defences were initially a ditch and a bank of earth, but walls were later built, with four gateways, and good internal roads were laid out as well.

As invaders, the Romans were naturally much-hated by the Britons. The Iceni tribe, for example, put up fierce resistance to their rule, and led by their queen Boudicca, they fought a number of major battles, including one at Stonea, not far from Cambridge. However, the occupying army generally brought order and stability to the area, and prosperity. They also gave local people protection – from other invaders. Across the North Sea, barbarians like the Angles and the Saxons, who came from the borderlands of present-day Denmark and Germany, saw Britain as ripe for conquest, but the presence of the Romans kept them at bay.

The situation changed at the start of the fifth century when Rome itself came under pressure from warlike hordes, such as the Vandals, Huns and Visigoths, who were on the rampage throughout Europe. To defend their empire, the Romans had no choice. They withdrew their troops from Britain, leaving the indigenous population to fend for itself.

With the well-drilled legions gone, the barbarians saw their chance, and they surged across the sea in a full-scale invasion. By the start of the seventh century, they controlled most of England, and in Cambridge, they had built homes on the eastern side of the River Cam, in the area where Great St Mary's Church is now. They had no liking for urban life, and few, if any, occupied any of the buildings of the Roman town, which was probably almost deserted. The Anglo-Saxons preferred to build their own rough timber huts, in little villages surrounded by farmland. They were also a very warlike people, and having violently subdued the local people, they fought bloody battles amongst themselves. Chieftains who had led the invasion became local kings, and then tried to increase their power by annexing the kingdoms of their weaker neighbours. One of the bigger kingdoms was East Anglia, and in the early years of the seventh century, it

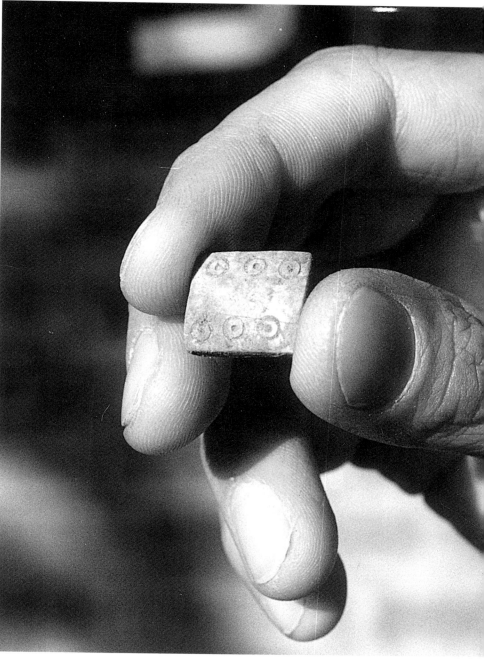

Roman remains – a checker piece, found in a dig near the city.

was embroiled in a war with another huge rival, Mercia, to the west. The River Cam formed part of the frontier between the two kingdoms, and the two sides are believed to have fought a number of battles along it. The Mercians emerged the victors, defeating the East Angles in 634.

In the eighth century, a new bridge was built across the river, probably by King Offa of Mercia, replacing one created hundreds of years before by the Romans. Like the Romans, Offa realised the strategic importance of the town. Its position made it easy to defend, and as far as commerce was concerned, it was ideal as a trade terminus for goods brought across the North Sea. The new bridge, not far from where the previous one had spanned the Cam, provided the town with a new name too, one that was very similar to the name it bears today. In the Anglo-Saxon Chronicle of 875, it is dubbed Granta Brycge, meaning the bridge over the River Granta, Granta being the ancient name for the Cam. The bridge also united the

two sides of the town, the one that had grown up from the old Roman settlement, and the other on the lower ground south and east of the river.

A new wave of invaders swept across East Anglia in the ninth century – the Danes. Like the Angles and Saxons before them, they burned and pillaged the countryside, and swarmed into Cambridge. *The Anglo Saxon Chronicle* describes how a trio of Danish kings, Godrum, Oscytel and Anwynd, arrived in the area 'with a great host, and remained there a year.' In fact, the Danes stayed a great deal longer than that, and settled mainly to the south of the city's modern-day Quayside. Archaeologists are convinced that is where they were partly by the presence of St Clement's Church – St Clement was a common church name in Danish settlements. Cambridge became part of the Danelaw, the territory in which Danish laws and customs were followed.

The Danelaw was reconquered by Edward the Elder in the early 10th century, and under him, the town expanded, with new churches, new businesses, and the King's Ditch, meant as a defence against further trouble. Boat traffic to the Fens from The Wash increased, and with it came merchants from the continent, keen to sell their wares and take local goods back with them. There were several mills alongside the river, and many farms in the surrounding area. So prosperous did Cambridge become that a mint was established, to feed demand for the King's coinage. Courts, called Shire Moots, also came into being, to keep the rising population under control. Cambridge became, and has remained ever since, the acknowledged county town.

In 1066, of course, there was yet another invader – William the Conqueror.

After defeating Harold's forces at the Battle of Hastings, William was crowned king at Westminster Abbey, but it was clear from the start of his reign that he would have to fight to keep the throne. He and his barons were hated foreigners on English soil. There were numerous uprisings against him, all of which he successfully stamped out, but he realised he would need to build his own defences if he was to maintain his grip on power. All over the country, he began to construct castles, of the motte and bailey type, as the military and administrative centres for his soldiers. Among them was Cambridge castle, finished in 1069. Today, little except the castle's earthworks remain, but in its day, it must have been an impressive fortress. Nearly 30 houses were knocked down to make way for it, and its position on high ground, together with the water-filled ditch that surrounded it, must have made it seem impregnable.

The gatehouse to Cambridge castle, built in the 13th century.

William installed a sheriff in the castle as his representative in the area, giving him the right to draw revenue from the town, and with jurisdiction over the populace. The first sheriff, Picot, was a much-hated figure. He was a greedy, arrogant man, who treated the townsfolk badly, seizing land when he needed it, and raising taxes when he felt like it. One chronicler at the time described him as 'a hungry lion, a ravening wolf, a filthy hog'. As well as taxes, he was entitled to requisition people's services too, ordering them to carry out tasks for him such as ploughing. This was highly unpopular in an area where farming was the biggest industry. Local peasants had to leave their own fields untilled while they discharged their duties on the sheriff's land. There was not much anyone could do about it. Picot was backed up by an armed force, and people could either do what he demanded, or face being thrown in jail.

One person who did stand up to the Normans, however, was the rebel leader Hereward the Wake. Famous for his great strength and swordsmanship, Hereward and his men refused to bow to William, and they made their stronghold on the Isle of Ely, an island of dry land in the middle of the boggy, marshy Fens. From there, they mounted raids on the surrounding countryside to fund their fight against the foreign king, including plundering nearby Peterborough Cathedral. The monks tried to defend themselves, but Hereward and his men were too strong. They burned the monks' houses and took all they could carry. The rebels were the last serious pocket of Saxon resistance against the invaders. In 1071, William decided

Hereward escaping from Ely, drawn in 1870.

enough was enough, and he sent an army to the Fens to track down Hereward and subdue him. The army had to use boats to get across the marshes, and with the assistance of the monks from Ely Abbey, who knew a secret pathway to their headquarters, the rebels were finally rounded up and killed – although Hereward himself is believed to have escaped.

This was not the end of the trouble. In 1087, William the Conqueror's son Rufus replaced him as King, but his brother Robert of Normandy disputed the succession, and the two ended up fighting each other for the crown of England. During one of Robert's campaigns against his brother, he marched into Cambridge – and torched the town. The same thing happened in the middle of the 12th century, when the English baron Geoffrey de Mandeville, rebelling against the authority of King Stephen, attacked Cambridge with a contingent of troops.

Although Cambridge occupied only a small area in Norman times – about 400 houses bounded by the ditch to the south and east, and the river to the north and west – it

St Bene't's Church, built about 1025.

St Giles Church.

survived such attacks, and continued to thrive. According to the *Domesday Book*, the nationwide audit of England's wealth ordered by William the Conqueror, its taxes amounted to 10 times the amount paid by any other settlement in the area. Its booming economy was given a further boost by Henry I, who became king in 1100 after the death of Rufus, William's successor. Henry ordered that ships could

Green lung – Jesus Green.

only unload their cargoes at the Cambridge hythes, effectively giving the town a monopoly on the river trade. New housing and business premises were built, on the land between what is now King's Parade and Trinity Street, then called High Street.

The leper chapel.

After the initial unrest it caused, the Norman Conquest led to a period of stability and security for Cambridge and towns like it. The population grew, agriculture became more intensively managed, and money began to replace bartering as the mainspring of the economy. In Cambridge, there were a large number of religious houses, a sure sign of prosperity. In ecclesiastical terms, the town was subsidiary to Ely's bishop, and there were no church buildings to rival the Ship of the Fens, Ely Cathedral. However, Cambridge did have several fine churches, among them the stone-towered Saxon church of St Bene't, built in about 1025, as well as a priory on the site of the present St Giles church, established as an act of piety by Sheriff Picot in 1092. In the early years of the 12th century, an Augustinian priory was built at Barnwell, and not many years later a Benedictine nunnery, dedicated to St Mary and St Radegund, was set up on the site of what is now Jesus College. The nunnery was granted the right to hold a fair every August, to augment its income, and it attracted backing from a number of rich benefactors, including King Malcolm of Scotland, who was also the Earl of Huntingdon. He gave money to the nuns, and 10 acres of land to help pay for their upkeep. Today, that land is a wonderful 'green lung' in the heart of Cambridge – Jesus Green and Midsummer Common.

There was also the leper hospital and chapel of St Mary Magdalene at Sturbridge, just off what is now Newmarket Road, near Cambridge United football ground. The chapel, founded in the mid 12th century, still stands and is one of the finest Norman buildings in existence in England, as well as the only surviving remnant of a leper hospital.

The appearance of all three of these religious houses helped to promote the eastward expansion of the town, along what is now Jesus Lane, and up Newmarket Road towards Newmarket. Houses were built on the higher land away from the riverbank. However, the coming of the religious orders also helped to stimulate the creation of something else, something that was to become the defining factor in the shaping of Cambridge over the next eight centuries.

It was started by a handful of men fleeing the wrath of the population in a town 100 miles away. The men were scholars from Oxford – and their arrival in the Fens led to the birth of the institution now acknowledged as the greatest seat of learning in the world: Cambridge University.

The Coming of the Clerkes

BY the beginning of the 13th century, Cambridge was one of the wealthiest parts of East Anglia. More and more land was being cleared for farming, and the town became the regional marketplace for the goods that were produced, mainly wheat, barley and wool. People came from far afield to sell or buy what was on offer, and there was a regular Saturday market, with eggs, butter, cheese, meat and fruit brought in from the surrounding countryside. The big local abbeys of Ely and Ramsey obtained much of their food supply from Cambridge, and crops were also exported to other parts of the country. On the edges of the town, to the west and east, were two vast arable fields, which were divided into strips and farmed by local people. There were also a number of smaller, agriculture-based settlements nearby. One of these was the royal manor of Chesterton, mentioned in the *Domesday Book* as Cestretone, meaning 'farm by the fortified place'.

Arable fields on the edge of Cambridge.

*Royal manor –
Chesterton, before it
became a suburb of
the city.*

Back in the 11th century it only had 24 families, but by the 13th century, due to
Cambridge's economic development, more than 160 people were paying taxes
there, according to the official records of the time, indicating a population of
between 700 and 800. Today, it is a densely-populated suburb of Cambridge.
Another farming community serving the town's needs was Cherry Hinton. It
included the manors of Nether Hall and Uphall, which before the Norman
conquest belonged to the mistress of King Harold, Edith the Fair, and as well as
farm land and the cherries from which its name derives, it also had quarries, useful

*Cambridge's first royal
charter, in 1201.*

for supplying the materials Cambridge needed for its new buildings. Trumpington was another key settlement, with more than 100 landholders by the end of the 13th century.

The Round Church.

As the economy grew, so did the number of people needed to fuel it, and the leading inhabitants were those who steered Cambridge's prosperity – the merchants, craftsmen, innkeepers, lawyers, and transport providers. The merchants were generally the richest people in the town, and for this reason, they also became its burgesses. A burgess was a free man, who had his own burgage, or plot, and who was entitled to farm strips of land. He was also allowed to sell goods in the town without paying any fees. The merchants formed themselves into associations called guilds, with the aim not only of encouraging trade, but controlling it too. By banding together, they became powerful enough to impose tolls on other merchants who came to Cambridge from elsewhere to sell their goods.

The more that Cambridge grew and prospered, the more its citizens wanted their freedom. Since the Norman conquest, they had been obliged to hand over a sizeable proportion of their income in taxes to the King, and to carry out services for their lords. Now, they wanted to keep more of their earnings for themselves, and like many other towns at the time, the burgesses decided to try to strike a bargain with the King to free them from their obligations. They wanted him to grant them a royal charter, spelling out their freedom, in exchange for a fixed sum of money and a yearly rent.

The man on the throne at the time was King John, and he was not averse to the idea of granting charters. In fact, he issued 70 of them in the 17 years he was ruler, between 1199 and 1216 – and Cambridge got one of the first of them, in 1201.

The charter granted many privileges to the burgesses, including the right to have a Guild of Merchants, whose members would be free of tolls throughout the King's lands. It was the first step along the road to Cambridge becoming more independent, and six years later, the King gave the town a second charter. This one stated that the town's contribution to the royal exchequer could be paid directly to the King, rather than through the sheriff. This was good news for the burgesses, because the sheriff had previously made a profit on the money he handled. Cutting out the middleman, and paying their dues direct into the royal coffers, saved the burgesses a lot of money. The town also got another important privilege – the right to elect a mayor, a further sign of its growing ability to govern itself.

King John's affection for money, and his views on religion, got him into a considerable amount of trouble. A few years after granting Cambridge its first charter, he quarrelled with the Pope, Innocent III, over who should be chosen as Archbishop of Canterbury. The Pope had picked his own candidate, Stephen Langton, an Englishman living at his court in Rome, but John refused to accept him. In 1208, in retaliation, the Pope put England under an interdict, which meant that all the churches had to be locked, and no services could be held, except baptism for infants and confession for the dying. In Cambridge, as elsewhere in the country, marriages could not take place, and no one could be buried in holy ground. This went on for six years, until the King relented, and the Pope lifted the ban.

Reach Fair – still in existence today. Evelyn Knowles, Cambridge's Mayor for 2000-01, tries out the amusements with city council chief executive Rob Hammond after opening the fair.

King John also faced a rebellion by his barons. Many had been forced to pay vast sums of money to him in dues, and they wanted a showdown. They drew up a list of grievances and presented them to the King, urging him to promise to keep the customs established by previous rulers. John rejected the demands, and in 1215, the barons gathered an army at Stamford and marched into London. John fled, and a few months later, the two sides met at Runnymede to talk peace. It was there that the most important document in English history, Magna Carta, was signed. It contained provisions formalising the relationship between the King and the barons, such as fixing the sum a baron had to pay when inheriting his father's lands. Most important of all, it also laid down regulations about justice. Until then, the King had the power to dispense justice as he wished, but it now became the law that no-one could be sent to jail or put to death without a fair trial.

After John's death, his nine-year-old son was crowned King Henry III, and a group of loyal barons ruled the country until the boy was old enough to take charge himself. Henry did not have a strong personality, and he allowed his French wife, Eleanor, to crowd his court with her friends and relatives, many of whom were given large estates. This caused another confrontation with the barons, led by the Earl of Leicester, Simon de Montfort, and in 1258, the King was forced to hand over much of his power to them.

In 1265, de Montfort held a Great Council, to which he invited not only nobles, but two burgesses from the leading towns, to represent ordinary people. This assembly was the forerunner of today's Parliament, with its House of Lords and House of Commons – and it was a sign of just how powerful the influence of merchants in wealthy towns like Cambridge had become in the affairs of the kingdom.

Later that same year, however, de Montfort's forces were confronted by an army led by Prince Edward, the King's eldest son, and were defeated in a bloody battle at Evesham. In Cambridgeshire, de Montfort's supporters, who had been dispossessed of their land and who called themselves The Disinherited, hid out in the Fens as Hereward had done, making forays into the surrounding countryside, and Cambridge itself, for food and other provisions. Those who got in their way were killed. Finally, the fugitives were flushed out by royal troops, who had to make pathways out of wickerwork to cross the marshy fens.

Although the merchants were now very powerful in Cambridge, there was one group of businessmen whose lives were turned upside down – the town's Jews. They had come to Cambridge soon after the Norman conquest, and had established a flourishing Jewish quarter, lending money not only to the merchants, but also to landowners who wanted to build homes in the surrounding area. The area where they lived was near the circular Church of the Holy Sepulchre, which was financially supported by the Knights Templar. Today it is known simply as the Round Church, and is one of the finest ecclesiastical buildings of its kind anywhere

Barges brought goods to Cambridge from King's Lynn.

in the country. Henry had enjoyed the Jews' financial backing too, but when he died and his son Edward came to the throne, his widow Eleanor persuaded the new King to decree that no Jew should dwell in any town where she owned property. Cambridge was such a town – and the royal order meant its Jewish population had to be deported en masse to nearby Huntingdon.

As well as the charters granted to Cambridge municipally, the town was lucky in being allowed to stage a number of fairs, which also made a contribution to its economic well-being. Unlike today's funfairs, which are generally for amusement, fairs in medieval times were for trading and commerce. The fun element only developed because they attracted large numbers of people, creating a market for food and entertainment. One popular gathering was Garlic Fair, the fair granted to the Benedictine nuns of St Mary and St Radegund about 1150, and held on what are now the grounds of Jesus College. Another fair took place at Reach, on the outskirts of Cambridge, at Rogation-tide, the three days leading up to Ascension Day. It is mentioned in the royal charter of 1201, although it had been up and running for many years before the charter came into being. Because of its river connections, Reach was a major centre for trade in East Anglia, linking with King's Lynn, or Lynn as it was then known, via the river at Cambridge. Ships plied back and forth, bringing leather goods, perfumes from abroad, spices, pottery, and a host of other items. Although Reach was on the edge of the town, the fair was thought of as a Cambridge event, and was opened by the Mayor – and still is today.

Another big gathering was Barnwell Fair, now known as Midsummer Fair, which is believed to have begun as early as the 12th century. It was less of a commercial fair than an occasion for entertainment, a traditional celebration of Midsummer Eve in June. In 1229, Henry III confirmed the right of the monks at Barnwell Abbey to hold it, but there were frequent rows between them and the burgesses about who should get the money from the tolls charged to stallholders. By the 18th century, it had developed as a trading fair, with earthenware the main commodity, which led to it also being called the Pot Fair.

Then there was Sturbridge Fair, which received an official charter from King John in 1210. The right to hold it was given to the leper hospital and chapel of St Mary Magdalene, and it took place on land between the river and Newmarket

Clare College, with its famous bridge.

Road, now called Stourbridge Common. This fair was originally only a few days in length, but it was to grow into one of the biggest and most important fairs in the whole of Europe, at one stage going on for more than a month. Like the fair at Reach, its enormous success was due to the river. Goods from abroad, including silks, furs and silverware, were switched to barges at King's Lynn and then unloaded at hythes stretching from Little St Mary's Lane to Magdalene Bridge.

While the early years of the 13th century were crucial to the future of Cambridge as a city, they were also the years that saw the birth of the institution that was to bring Cambridge worldwide fame – Cambridge University.

There is a legend that a Spanish prince, Cantaber, founded a city on the River Cante, to which he brought philosophers and astronomers from Athens. Another legend says the university was founded in AD 637 by Sigebert, King of the East Angles, and that King Arthur gave it a charter in 531. In reality, it was a group of clerkes, or scholars, from Cambridge's great modern-day rival, Oxford, who got the university going – and it began because of a murder.

Oxford University had been in existence since the 12th century, from about 1149. Because of their relatively privileged lifestyles, and the pressure their presence put on accommodation in the town, there was a great deal of friction between the Oxford scholars and the townsfolk there. When a woman was found killed, popular suspicion fell on the clerkes. Two of them were arrested for her murder, and were hanged by the town authorities. In protest, the university went into voluntary suspension, and most of its scholars left the town, to try to resume their studies elsewhere. Many went to the Continent, to join European universities, such as Paris – but one group came to Cambridge, in 1209.

Most of the scholars were clerics, and Cambridge was attractive to them because it had so many religious houses, such as Barnwell Priory, as well as a number of schools. These were generally run by monks, friars or priests, and consisted of a single teacher and a class of 20 or 30 boys. Latin was the main subject, both as a written and spoken language, and although discipline was tough – pupils were regularly birched if they got their lessons wrong – the young people enjoyed learning, and wanted to find out about other subjects as well, such as arithmetic, geometry and astronomy. To the displaced Oxford clerkes, they represented a ready-made educational market.

Gonville and Caius College.

At first, the teachers and their students held classes anywhere they could find accommodation. The fledgling university had no buildings of its own, and there were as yet no colleges, so tutorials took place in rented rooms. Within a few years, however, a form of graduation had been established, as well as a system for licensing the teachers, who were called masters. The university also had a head, the Chancellor.

In 1229, Henry III invited the students who had gone into self-enforced exile at the University of Paris to return to England, and resume their studies in Cambridge, which many did. A couple of years later, the king issued four writs referring to how the new university should be run, one of which made it a rule that a student could not remain in the university unless he was under the tuition of a licensed master. Another related to 'unruly clerkes'. Any who misbehaved would be reported to the Bishop of Ely and punished by the sheriff, it warned.

There was certainly a need for discipline. The students were constantly causing trouble, brawling amongst themselves, and getting into fights with the townsfolk. Many nurtured private vendettas against fellow students, and some even turned to crime. On one occasion, in the early 1260s, a group of four clerkes plotted to burgle the house of a Cambridge vintner. However, they were betrayed to the sheriff by other students, and were caught in the act of breaking in. The punishment, as it was for many crimes in medieval times, was draconian – they were all beheaded. At about the same time, there was a violent clash between two different groups of students, in which the townspeople joined. Houses were burned and plundered, and some of the university's records, the symbol of its power and prestige, were destroyed. The trouble got so bad that the King had to intervene personally, and three judges were appointed to sort things out. The result was more executions – 16 townspeople were put to death. A number of students decided to leave Cambridge, and went to Northampton, with the idea of starting up a new university there, but the attempt was blocked by the King, on the grounds that it might harm the status of the established universities if another were to be founded.

The subjects pursued by the students were grammar, logic and rhetoric, and arithmetic, music, geometry and astronomy, leading to degrees of bachelor and master. All the teaching was done by masters who had themselves been educated at the university, and who had then been licensed by the university as teachers. Each student had to enrol with a master in a process that was called matriculation – the student's name had to appear on the master's matriculus, or roll. After examinations – not sit-down, written affairs like today, but oral disputations in which the candidates discussed a series of questions or theses – they were able to graduate into the different degrees, or grades, of university membership.

The teaching body became known as the Regent Masters, and it appointed two representatives to act and speak on its behalf, the Proctors. They kept the university's accounts, and supervised its rules and regulations, the statutes, which they carried with them in large, leather-bound books. The earliest known version of these statutes, written down in the mid-13th century, is in the Vatican library.

As the number of students grew, the colleges came into being, principally as places where teaching could take place, and where the students and their teachers could live.

Today, the colleges still fulfil that role, working alongside the university. Each college has its own self-governing body, its own rules and regulations, and its own income. The university provides a range of central facilities for the students and staff to use, such as lecture halls and research laboratories. Every student who comes to Cambridge must win a place at one of the colleges – but it is the university which lays down the admission qualifications for undergraduates, and which confers degrees.

There is still a figurehead, the Chancellor – at present the Duke of Edinburgh – but there is also a chief executive-style full-time official who supervises its day-to-day running, the Vice-Chancellor. Each college has a Master, Mistress or President.

The oldest college in Cambridge is Peterhouse, founded in 1284 by Hugh de Balsham, who was to become Bishop of Ely. Originally it was just two small houses, and its students were all in training for the priesthood. There were 14 Fellows, eight scholars, and a Master. Today, the college has extensive buildings in Trumpington Street, next to the university's art museum, the Fitzwilliam. Peterhouse was followed a few years later by another tiny college called King's Hall, which only had one teacher and 12 young students, and then a third college, Michaelhouse, was founded in 1324. Neither of these colleges, King's Hall or Michaelhouse, exists any more – both have since been absorbed into Trinity College, created by King Henry VIII more than two centuries later.

Five more colleges were founded in the 14th century. First there was Clare, established in 1338, and which now has the oldest college bridge across the River Cam. Next came Pembroke, in 1347, and a year later, Gonville and Caius. It was originally started by a priest, Edmund Gonville, but was further endowed by Dr John Caius, physician to Edward VI, in 1557. Then there was Trinity Hall in 1350, founded by another bishop, William Bateman of Norwich, again mainly to train young men for the priesthood. Finally, Corpus Christi College was established, in

*Great St Mary's
Church was used for
university ceremonies.*

1352. It was, and still is, the college with the closest links to Cambridge as a town. Many of the colleges were founded by kings, queens or churchmen, but Corpus Christi had the distinction of being established by two town guilds, Corpus Christi and the Blessed Virgin Mary, under the patronage of the Duke of Lancaster. Like other early colleges in Cambridge, it was started as a chantry – a side chapel to an existing church, with a wealthy benefactor paying the stipend of a priest who would be able to offer Mass for the benefactor's soul or for his dead relatives. The material used to build much of it, appropriately, was local clunch, quarried at Cherry Hinton.

The university itself continued to have few buildings of its own until the late 14th century. It used parish churches, such as Great St Mary's, for its degree ceremonies, and stored its records there as well. Then it began to acquire property on the site known today as Senate House Hill, and put up a group of buildings there, which in those days were called the Schools, and which are now known as the Old Schools. The buildings included teaching rooms, a chapel, a library and the University Treasury.

Cambridge was not the only university in the town – Oxford had a foothold too.

The Other Place's Merton College had an offshoot in Cambridge called the School of Pythagoras, formerly the house of a rich citizen, the town's first Mayor Hervey fitz Eustace. Merton bought it to accommodate some of its scholars who had fled the trouble in Oxford.

At the request of King Edward II, the Pope, John XII, formally recognised Cambridge in 1318 as a Studium Generale, a general school, which could take scholars not just from the immediate vicinity, but from anywhere in the world. The Pope's blessing for the university also meant that its scholars had the right to lecture throughout Christendom.

In fact, many of the university's first students were not from far flung parts, but came from East Anglia itself, and from the North-East of England. Most were of yeoman stock, not from the landed gentry, who at the time felt they had no real need of the education a university had to offer. The students were young – far younger than they are today. The majority were between 15 and 17, and some were only 14. Sometimes their upkeep was paid for by a rich patron, in the form of an ecclesiastical living. The poorer ones were even granted licence to beg. They lived two or three to a room, initially in rented lodgings, and later, as the colleges were founded, in hostels. Conditions were pretty poor. Most of the rooms were without an open fire, and sleeping accommodation often had to be shared. Fires were usually only lit

Peterhouse, Cambridge's oldest college.

at Christmas, and the students were forbidden to indulge in frivolous pursuits. Card games were banned, for example, on the grounds that they would distract the young men from their studies. The students were also not allowed to wear rings on their fingers, or coloured shoes, and they had to wear gowns, which were mainly black, but which also contained colours or stripes to denote which college they came from.

To escape their cold, grim lodgings, and the rigid discipline of academic life, the students headed for the warmth of Cambridge's taverns, and it was often there, after liberal quantities of ale had been consumed, that trouble broke out between them and the townsfolk. Right from the time it came into existence, the university had attempted to secure its position by demanding that the town recognised its superiority. For example, in 1317, a royal charter came into force which stated that Cambridge's mayor and bailiffs, on taking office, must swear to 'maintain the privileges' of the university. Such arrogance was guaranteed to cause resentment, and there were many riots as a result. In 1322, townsfolk laid siege to the hostels, attacked the students living there, and killed a priest.

The coming of the clerkes had begun an era that was to bring great prosperity, and international fame, to Cambridge – but it also split the town in two.

Kings and Queens

LIFE was hard at the start of the 1300s, and it became a great deal harder as the century wore on. In 1348, residents in Cambridge heard about a terrifying plague that was sweeping the continent, killing thousands of people. Those struck down by it developed large swellings under their armpits and between their legs, and then they began vomiting, and spitting blood. Within three days, most victims had died.

The mysterious disease was bubonic plague – the Black Death. No one believed it would reach England, but within a year it had, on merchant ships, carried by fleas in the fur of the black rats lurking below decks.

It is not known exactly how many people lived in Cambridge at the time, but the Hundred Rolls survey of the late 13th century had revealed 535 dwelling houses, together with 17 churches, 76 shops and stalls, and five large farms – a sizeable

Poorer than it appeared: the Black Death and failed harvests hit Cambridge's economy.

population. The Black Death, when it arrived, claimed the lives of about half the town's inhabitants. Three masters from St John's Hospital died, as did the Prior of Barnwell, most of the scholars at King's Hall, and almost the entire parish of All Saints, near the castle. Many of the dead were buried in mass graves. It was not the only outbreak,

University chest – official documents were kept in chests like this one in the Old Schools.

either. The plague returned several times in the years that followed, claiming many hundreds more lives.

Cambridge had been a well-heeled market town, but a number of factors had combined to put the brakes on its economy. The arrival of the scholars, and the birth of the university, gave trade an initial lift, but many of the students who came to the town were from poor families, and had very little money to spend. In 1346, asked by the royal exchequer to make a contribution towards the costs of the Battle of Crecy, Cambridge actually pleaded poverty, and told the King it had 'too many beggars and scholars' on its streets. Early in the 14th century, the corn harvest failed on several occasions, a major blow to what was still a mostly agrarian area. On a number of occasions, local men had also been drafted into the army, to fight in France and in Scotland – and taxes kept going up to meet the cost of the conflicts.

The Black Death plunged the town and county into even deeper crisis. The plague denuded the countryside of workers, and those who remained felt they

Magdalene College today.

Lady Margaret Beaufort – copied by Dolores de Fischer from the original, which hangs in the National Portrait Gallery.

deserved more pay because they were working harder. Wage demands began to spiral, not just in Cambridge but nationwide, and in response a law was passed declaring that wages should remain at pre-plague levels. Then a new tax, the poll tax, was introduced in 1380, payable by everyone over the age of 15. For poorer people, it amounted to only 4d, but that was more than a day's earnings. In Cambridge, where townsfolk already felt bitter and resentful about the local taxes they had to pay, it was the final straw.

People were also angry at the university's interference in the running of the town. The number of students and teachers in Cambridge was growing, and they needed lodgings. Because they were generally strapped for cash, they wanted to pay the lowest rent they could, and as little as possible for their victuals – food, drink, and candles. The university insisted that it should be able to have some control over these prices, and its royal connections ensured that it got its way.

Things came to a head in 1381, the year of the Peasants' Revolt. In Essex and Kent, thousands of people rebelled against the Crown and refused to pay their taxes. They armed themselves with swords, longbows and scythes and marched to London, led by Wat Tyler. When they reached the capital, they went on the rampage, looting and burning. The King, Richard II, was still only a 14-year-old boy, and the rebels had no quarrel with him. Their anger was directed at the lords, lawyers and churchmen who were responsible for putting up the taxes. Many of them were rounded up and beheaded. Richard had no choice but to meet the

King's College.

peasants, and he did so, reassuring them that their demands would be met – but after they left London and went back to their homes, he broke the promise he had made, and sent soldiers into the countryside to root out the ringleaders of the revolt and punish them. All over the South-East, peasants were rounded up and hanged on roadside gallows, as a warning to others.

During the revolt, Cambridge was one of the main trouble spots. Mobs of townspeople ran amok. A judge was beheaded, a ship on the river was plundered, and Barnwell Priory, the symbol of church authority, was attacked. Corpus Christi College, which had substantial land-owning interests in the town, was set alight. During Sunday Mass at Great St Mary's Church, a mob burst in and smashed open a chest containing papers and other items belonging to the university. After burning the contents, they

King's College Chapel.

went to a house nearby and broke open a second university chest, full of books and documents. In other towns where trouble had flared, it had generally involved only peasants, rebelling against the town authorities and local landowners. In Cambridge, because of the unpopularity of the university, the Mayor and burgesses not only sided with the peasants, they were also the mob ringleaders. After breaking open the university chests, the Mayor forced the masters and scholars to sign two deeds, the first renouncing all privileges granted to the university by the kings of England 'since the beginning of the world', and promising to conform to the law and customs of the borough of Cambridge; and the second promising to abandon 'all actions real and personal' against the burgesses. The deeds were sealed with the common seal of the university, and the seals of all the colleges, and the university and colleges then had to surrender all their charters of privileges, which were piled up in the market place and set on fire. As the parchments crackled and burned, one chronicler reports, an old woman tossed the ashes into the air, screaming: 'Away with the learning of the clerks, away with it.'

*The Mathematical
Bridge at Queens'.*

The citizens' euphoria at freeing themselves from what they regarded as the tyranny of the university was short-lived. Troops, led by the Bishop of Norwich, arrived within a few days and quelled the rioting. Many of the townspeople who had played a leading part in the trouble were hanged. The deeds the academics had been compelled to sign were later formally quashed by Parliament, and a year later, the King gave the university yet another royal charter – a charter that really rubbed salt into the town's wounds.

The charter of 1382 permitted the university jurisdiction over the 'assize of bread, wine and beer', and 'assay of weights and measures'. It meant the university,

Queens' College.

not the town, could now set the prices for food and drink, and it gave the university the right to check the scales and other measures used by local traders, to make sure they were not trying to cheat. In return for these privileges, the university had to pay the King a yearly fee – £10 – and the townspeople were forbidden to interfere. Of course, these powers had previously been vested in the Mayor and the town Corporation, and their removal deepened the enmity between Cambridge and its university. Remarkably, the university retained the right to set prices and check weights and measures until the middle of the 19th century, and in the intervening years, there were numerous instances of trouble between the two sides as a result.

A second royal charter the following year allowed the university even more say in how the town was run. It gave the Chancellor 'cognizance of all personal pleas, trespasses against the peace, and misprisions within the town and suburbs...where a master, scholar, or scholar's servant, or common minister of the University should be a party'. Effectively, this meant the university could run its own courts.

It could impose fines, imprison offenders in the castle, and order temporary or permanent banishment. The only cases it did not have jurisdiction over were incidents involving murder or serious violence, which were reserved for the King's justices to deal with.

As time went on, and the provisions of this new charter were implemented, there were many miscarriages of university justice. Sometimes, for example, the university status of those deemed to have been affected by a crime was dubious to say the least. In the end, it was yet another cause of discord between town and gown.

Bolstered by its new-found

The Backs today.

Cricket on Parker's Piece.

authority, the university expanded rapidly during the 15th and 16th centuries. Eleven more colleges were founded, and a number of hostels were built to house the students flocking to Cambridge.

In 1428, Magdalene College came into existence, originally known as Buckingham College. Then, in the 1440s, Christ's was started. It too had another name at first, Godshouse, and was refounded in 1505 by Lady Margaret Beaufort, one of the university's earliest and greatest benefactors. She was the mother of Henry VII, and as well as establishing Christ's, she founded lectureships, made endowments, and transformed the old hospital of St John into St John's College, in 1511.

The college which visitors to Cambridge instantly associate with the city, King's, was begun in 1441. It was the brainchild of Henry VI, then just a young man, who also founded Eton College about the same time. Henry was a very religious man, and he wanted the college and its magnificent chapel to be a memorial to his piety.

St Catharine's College, founded in 1473.

It is doubtful whether Cambridge residents shared his opinion. A large area of land had to be cleared, and scores of houses demolished – about a quarter of the town – to make room for the new college. Of Henry's elaborate plans, however, only the chapel was built, and even that was not completed until more than 70 years later. Henry's successors – Edward IV, Richard III, Henry VII and Henry VIII – all had a hand in it, and the main fabric was finished in 1515, delayed many times because of the political upheaval associated with the Wars of

Trinity College, founded by Henry VIII.

the Roses. For many years, college members lived in one small court to the north of the chapel until other college buildings, including the hall range, porters' lodge and screen, were finally built, together with other buildings to the west and south of the chapel.

The chapel is, of course, the jewel in Cambridge's architectural crown. Its wonderful stone, fan-vaulted ceiling measures nearly 290 feet long, and soars 80 feet in height. Its windows, created by English and Flemish craftsmen between 1515 and 1531, are among the most beautiful in the world, telling stories from the Old and New Testaments. There is also the unique Rood Screen, erected between 1533 and 1536, which has the initials of Henry VIII and Anne Boleyn on it, the carved choir stalls famous around the world due to the broadcasting of the Christmas Eve carol service, and the altar, with Rubens' painting The Adoration of the Magi, given as a gift to King's in the early 1960s.

In honour of its founder, King Henry, the college still sends a sheaf of roses to the Tower of London every year on the anniversary of his death, and Eton sends a sheaf of white lilies. This has happened every year since 1471.

Not long after work began on King's College, Henry VI's wife and queen, Margaret of Anjou, authorised the founding of another college alongside the river, Queen's. Construction of the buildings, not in stone but in the red brick that was to be used for a number of other colleges, had already started a couple of years earlier. The scheme was the inspiration of Andrew Docket, Rector of St Botolph's church, and principal of St Bernard's Hostel, and he intended to call the new institution St Bernard's College. However, the queen took over the scheme 'to laud and honneure of sexe feminine', and it was subsequently named Queen's. When she was forced to flee the country during the Wars of the Roses, Elizabeth Woodville, queen of Henry's successor Edward IV, gave the college her patronage, and saw the project through to completion. Having been created by two queens, the college's name was duly pluralised, and renamed Queens'. Like King's, it too has something that is known to tourists the world over – the famous Mathematical Bridge, said to have been constructed on geometric principles entirely without nails, but since taken apart and rebuilt.

As well as their marvellous buildings, King's and Queens' played a part in providing Cambridge with another of its scenic attractions. While they were becoming established, the two colleges had acquired land between the river and the

town's West Fields, meadows that had been used for many years for grazing. In the early 17th century, St John's and Trinity were to acquire the rest of this pasture, called Long Green, giving the colleges control of the wide strip of land next to Queen's Road. There was no altruism involved. The colleges wanted the land, which bordered the river and became known as the Backs, for their own gardens, and to provide secluded walks for their members. Today, it is virtually as it was all those centuries ago, its colleges, punts, and tree-lined banks the focus of every tourist's camera.

It was another land deal that gave Cambridge its green space in the heart of the modern city, Parker's Piece. Trinity College was keen to build on Garret Hostel Green, and the lease on the land was actually in the possession of one of the college's own cooks, Edward Parker. The college persuaded the town to do a lease swap, and in exchange for being allowed to build on the land it wanted, it provided the town with an arable field at Barnwell, which was appropriately named after Parker. Today, Parker's Piece is used for community events and cricket matches, and by local schools, but in the 17th century, it was actually ploughed, and then later used as grazing land.

The Great Court at Trinity College.

Emmanuel College.

Two other colleges were established towards the end of the 15th century – St Catharine's, founded in 1473 by the then Provost of King's College, Robert Woodlark; and Jesus College. The convent of St Mary and St Radegund had stood on the Jesus site since the 12th century, but by 1496, it was virtually empty – only two nuns remained. The Bishop of Ely, John Alcock, dissolved the convent, and set up the college in its place.

Trinity College, the biggest and richest of Cambridge's colleges, was founded by Henry VIII in 1546. It began as two smaller colleges, King's Hall and Michaelhouse, and there was also a hostel on the site. Initially, these existing buildings were used for the new college, and others were then added. In the latter years of the 16th century, Trinity's master, Thomas Nevile, cleared the buildings in the area between the two former colleges, and created a spectacular open space, the Great Court –

St John's College.

the largest court of its kind, and one of the most unusual too. Ruth Mellanby, a writer about Cambridge, describes it in this way: 'It is not a regular space bounded by sides of equal dimensions. No corner is a right angle, no side is straight, the fountain is not in the middle, and the gates are out of centre. Yet the whole is most pleasing, and it is the largest and most beautiful court in either university.'

In 1584, another former religious house, the Dominican friary off St Andrew's Street, became a college too – Emmanuel. Its founder was Sir Walter Mildmay, then the Chancellor of the Exchequer. Twelve years later, the former Franciscan friary nearby also became a college, Sidney Sussex, named after the Earl of Sussex by his widow, Lady Frances Sidney. Its most famous student, who arrived there two decades after the college was established, was a man who

Memorial to Thomas
Cranmer, Jesus
College.

John Fisher, with kind
permission of the
Master and Fellows of
Christ's College.

Far left: William Lee,
immortalised in a
window at Christ's
College.

was to play a crucial role in the history of Cambridge, and the nation – Oliver Cromwell.

The new colleges consolidated Cambridge's growing reputation as one of the leading international academies. For many years, the East Anglian university had been considerably smaller than Oxford, and was regarded in Europe as very much its junior. By the end of the 15th century, however, student numbers in Cambridge matched those in Oxford, and in the 16th century, Cambridge's profile as a place of learning and scholarship reached new heights.

The architect of much of the university's growth at this time was John Fisher, its Chancellor from 1504. He had been a member of the household of Lady Margaret Beaufort, and evidence suggests it was he who persuaded her to found Christ's College, and he who brought to fruition her final benefaction, which led to the founding of St John's College. He himself contributed £1,000 to the cost – a huge sum in those days.

Fisher was also a personal friend of one of the leading European intellectuals of the time, Erasmus. He convinced the Dutch scholar to come to Cambridge, to lecture in Greek and Divinity. Erasmus arrived in 1511, basing himself at Queens' College, and while in Cambridge, he developed his humanist ideas and laid the foundations for some of his greatest works, *Novum Instrumentum*, and *St Jerome*, both of which were published in 1516. He also set about translating the New

Testament from its original Greek into Latin, and his presence in Cambridge not only enhanced the university's reputation, but also raised its standards of teaching.

This was the time of the English Reformation – the period of religious turbulence that led to the break-up of the medieval church, and the creation of Protestant and Anglican churches alongside Roman Catholic ones. In 1517, Martin Luther, a Professor of the Old Testament at Wittenberg University, spelled out his doubts about what were then universally-accepted beliefs, such as the concept of salvation. His views caused fury in the Roman Catholic Church, and in 1520, he was excommunicated. His books were banned, and in many places, publicly burned, including on the streets of Cambridge, where the papal condemnation of Luther had been posted on the doors of the university's schools.

Not everyone in Cambridge, however, rejected the German professor's ideas, nor agreed with the need to suppress them. A number of academics held meetings in a Cambridge public house, the White Horse Tavern, near King's College, to discuss Luther's books (enterprising local booksellers had smuggled some in) and engage in theological debate. The meetings became so frequent that the tavern got the nickname 'Little Germany', and among those who took part were Matthew Parker, the Master of Corpus Christi College, William Tyndale, the famous Bible translator, the preacher Hugh Latimer, and Robert Barnes, prior of the Augustinian friars. Also there on many occasions was Thomas Cranmer, a Fellow of Jesus College – the man who was to become Archbishop of Canterbury not too long afterwards.

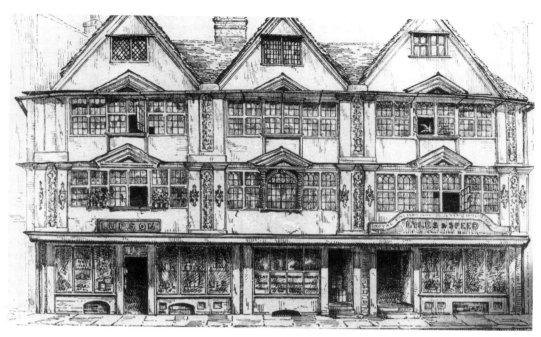

The King, Henry VIII, was a staunch Catholic, and he had written an impassioned Defence of the Seven Sacraments, for which the Pope had given him the title Defender of the Faith. Henry believed that Cambridge University's top brains should be drafted into the battle against Luther's ideas, and he enlisted Fisher, a Catholic bishop, to the cause. Fisher duly spoke out strongly against Luther, and wrote books condemning the Reformation, which bore the royal coat of arms. His support for the King, however, backfired. When the Pope refused to allow Henry a divorce from his ageing Spanish wife, Catherine of Aragon, the King was furious. He turned against the Papacy, and demanded that those around him did the same. Fisher would not do so, and in 1535, both he and Thomas More, who had helped to write Henry's *Defence of the Seven Sacraments*, were executed for refusing to swear to the King's supremacy over the church. Cambridge's church reformers suffered a similar fate. Barnes was burned at the stake in 1540, and Tyndale went to Germany and began publishing his work there, but was later executed after being arrested in Brussels.

Cranmer was one of Henry's few trusted confidants, and he had worked hard on the King's behalf to secure the annulment of the marriage to Catherine of Aragon. Despite his anti-papist views, the King appointed him Archbishop of Canterbury, but when the King died, Cranmer was accused of treason, thrown in jail, and also died at the stake, in 1556.

University people were not the only ones to suffer during the Reformation. The parish priest of St Clement's, for example, injudiciously revealed his loathing of the King's religious beliefs one evening in a Cambridge pub. One of his parishioners denounced him to the authorities, and he was promptly arrested and imprisoned.

Before Henry came to the throne, Cambridge had been known for its religious houses – the Dominicans in St Andrew's Street, the Franciscans at the corner of Jesus Lane, the Carmelites near Queens' College, the Augustinians, Luther's order, between Bene't Street and Free School Lane, and the Benedictines on the edge of the city. The dissolution of the monasteries by Henry saw many of these turned to a new use – as colleges.

Jesus College – a convent was formerly on the site.

In addition to the religious turmoil of the Tudor years, there was political upheaval as well, and Cambridge was again in the thick of it. In Cambridge, as elsewhere in the country, the enclosure of land was taking place. Common land once available to all was being parcelled up and made the property of individuals, some of them the town's burgesses. The university had also taken control of a substantial amount of land which used to have common grazing rights. Some people were getting rich as a result, and the poor were being deprived of their meagre livelihood. In 1549, a rebellion broke out against these practices in Norfolk, led by a Wymondham farmer, Robert Kett. Leading citizens were taken prisoner, and were held in camps. The trouble inevitably spread to Cambridge, where about a hundred protesters ripped up fences around some of the enclosed land near the town, and hurled them into the River Cam. In Norfolk, the revolt was quelled by the Duke of Northumberland, John Dudley, who massacred those who had taken part in it. Then in Cambridge, in a rare show of solidarity, the burgesses and the university temporarily set aside their differences and took action together to halt the trouble, executing a number of the people responsible.

Dudley made an appearance in Cambridge soon afterwards. When Henry VIII's young successor Edward VI died, the Duke was determined to see his daughter-in-law, Lady Jane Grey, become Queen. In 1553, he raised an army and set off to intercept the woman most people believed should really be on the throne, Edward's half-sister Mary, as she travelled towards London. The attempt was a failure. The Privy Council declared Mary was the rightful Queen, and by the time Northumberland reached Cambridge, most of his soldiers had deserted, and he had to acknowledge his defeat, which he did publicly in the town's marketplace. He was later executed as a traitor.

Queen Mary, although only on the throne for six years, became known as Bloody Mary because of the violent religious repression that took place during her reign. Hundreds of people were rounded up, accused of heresy, and burned at the stake, the method of execution deemed most suitable for cleansing their souls. Among those to die at this time was Nicholas Ridley, the master of Pembroke College, who had been outspoken in support of Lady Jane Grey, and Hugh Latimer, the Cambridge don who had attended the 'Little Germany' meetings 35 years before. Now an old man, he was taken into the marketplace in Oxford, and burned. As the flames rose around him, he displayed the same immense courage as many of those who had died before him for their beliefs, crying out the famous words: 'We shall this day light such a candle as shall never be put out.' Cambridge had its pyres of death too. Protestant John Hullier, a former chaplain at King's

College, was handed over by the university authorities to the town – and burned at the stake on Jesus Green. In another bizarre act, the bones of Calvinist Martin Bucer, who had come to Cambridge in 1549 as Regius Professor of Divinity but had died two years later, were dug up and ceremonially burned too.

Matthew Parker, reproduced courtesy of Corpus Christi College.

When Mary died in 1558, Elizabeth became Queen, beginning a 40-year reign that was to bring unity back to the country, and to give unprecedented encouragement to the arts. It was the age of Shakespeare, and his Cambridge-educated contemporaries like Edmund Spenser, writer of *The Faerie Queene*, and the poet and dramatist Christopher Marlowe, who is believed to have begun writing his plays while still a student at Corpus Christi College.

Two other Cambridge men were the Queen's most trusted lieutenants. One was William Cecil, her wise and loyal First Secretary, who was also Chancellor of Cambridge University. He was a key figure in the Elizabethan government, and much respected by the Queen, who put a high value on his honesty and administrative skills. The Queen and her counsellor only fell out once, when having persuaded Elizabeth to sign the death warrant of Mary Queen of Scots, Cecil had the sentence carried out before the Queen had decided whether she wanted the execution to go ahead. Elizabeth's other great confidant was Matthew Parker, Master of Corpus Christi. He had been chaplain to Elizabeth's mother, Anne Boleyn, and when Elizabeth became Queen she made him Archbishop of Canterbury. In keeping with the spirit of learning at the time, Parker was a literary man. He sponsored a new translation of the Bible into English, and was a passionate book collector. In 1568, the Queen gave him licence to seek out 'auncient recordes or monumentes' from the former libraries of the monasteries suppressed by Henry VIII, and from the old cathedral priories, and he set about the task with vigour. He collected manuscripts of huge importance from all over the country, and the books he gathered were the first major antiquarian collection ever assembled in England, long before Thomas Bodley began the collection that was to become the Bodleian in Oxford, or Robert Cotton began to collect the material that formed the basis of the British Library. Parker secured very early copies of the Bible, and one of his most important acquisitions was a Gospel Book sent by Augustine to Gregory the Great in the sixth century – which as a symbol of religion, history and literacy is probably the single most important book in England. Corpus Christi still has many of the books he collected, in its Parker Library, including the oldest known manuscript of the *Anglo-Saxon Chronicle*, the most valuable historical record of early English history. Parker's determination to find the books and manuscripts he wanted earned him a nickname, which is still applied today to anyone with an excessive sense of curiosity – Nosey Parker.

The Elizabethan delight in literature rubbed off on Cambridge's economy in the 16th century. Bookstalls began to appear in the town, most of them concentrated

Examinations in progress at Trinity College.

around the market area. One, now the Cambridge University Press shop in Trinity Street, claims to be the oldest bookshop in England. Cambridge also played a part in two of the great inventions of the Elizabethan age. Sir John Harington, a poet and translator, whose godmother was the Queen, was banished from London for reading salacious stories to young ladies of the court. While in exile, he came up with the idea of a flushable toilet, in 1597. His image is immortalised in a stained glass window at his old college, Christ's. Another Cambridge inventor was the Reverend William Lee, who designed a very early knitting machine, in 1589. It introduced a technique called frame-work knitting, which used a separate needle for each loop, instead of casting all the loops onto a single needle, as in hand-knitting.

During Elizabeth's reign, the university set up a well-organised system of matriculation and graduation, dividing students into three categories – noblemen, pensioners and sizars. Noblemen paid high fees, but were entitled to proceed to their degrees without having to sit proper examinations. They wore gowns and caps and were sometimes given the status of Fellow-commoners – students who took their meals, or commons, at the Fellows' table. The Fellows were the colleges' senior members. Pensioners were the equivalent of the middle-classes, paying fees to the colleges for their board and lodging, but dependent on passing exams to earn their degrees. Sizars were the poorest students, who had to earn their keep by performing menial tasks, such as waiting on table, cleaning the courts, and helping in the library.

The colleges varied in size from about 20 Fellows and students at St Catharine's in 1564 to more than 300 at Trinity. College plays, in Latin, were the main form of entertainment, but only in colleges where there were enough students. Most dramas required a large cast. Many students, much to the annoyance of the university authorities, frequently sought other diversions. They spent a lot of time in the town's inns and hostelries, took part in public entertainments, such as bear-baiting, and even played an early version of football. The first proper rules for the game were drawn up in Cambridge, but in those days, it was very much a free-for-all, with no limit on the number of players. The main intention was not to score goals, but to injure the opposition. One match, between students and villagers from Chesterton, ended in a pitched battle, with the two teams clubbing each other with wooden staves. From then on, students were barred by the university authorities from taking part in such games. This kind of recreation was considered a big threat to the young men's 'deportment', as was drinking. In 1564, the Queen gave the Chancellor the right to licence alehouses, so that it could force them to ensure that students were refused entry. Within a few years of the university beginning to exercise its power in this respect, much to the disgruntlement of students and townsfolk alike, the number of taverns had dropped from 80 to about 30.

Petty Cury was the street where many of the main inns were, and as well as patronising them for recreational purposes, many students actually lodged in them, just as law students in London lived in the Inns of Court. Most colleges had no refectories, so the inns served as restaurants for the students, as well as for local people, market traders and travellers. That is why the street got its unusual name – Petty Cury means 'little cookery'.

Queen Elizabeth paid a visit to Cambridge in 1564, part of a summer tour of the country. She was still young, in her early 30s, and only six years into her reign, and the town was agog at the news that she was to spend three nights at King's College. Detailed instructions were sent from the court to William Cecil, telling him to order the university's 1,200 members to cut short their vacation and return to Cambridge early, so they could line the streets when Elizabeth arrived. As she passed by, the people must shout Vivat Regina, Long Live the Queen, while 'lowly kneeling', the university was informed. There were 14 colleges at the time, and each made preparations to accommodate sections of the royal party and its courtiers. The streets were sanded, the cross in the market area was given a new coat of paint, and extra food and ale was laid in.

On a warm day in August, the Queen arrived. The royal procession made its way from Haslingfield to Grantchester, and then to Newnham, where the Queen was met by the Mayor. Crowds flocked to see her as she rode into Cambridge dressed in a gown of black velvet, and a hat spangled with gold. She was presented with a silver cup by the town, containing 40 gold coins, bells rang out, and there was a real party atmosphere. After the misery, violence and repression of the years that had gone before, people felt a new era had dawned.

In 1570, the university asked the Queen if it could have its own MP in Parliament. She said no, but the request was later granted by her successor, King James, in 1604, just after her reign came to an end. Worried by yet another example of power accruing to the university, the town later petitioned the new King for Cambridge to be given the status of city. However, the plea was turned down when university officials warned James that elevating Cambridge in this way would pose a threat to the university's privileges. The university told the King: 'The home of the Muses could gain no additional honour from the plebeian title of city.'

Cambridge's ancient coat of arms.

The town did get a coat of arms, however, in 1575, thanks to the efforts of the Mayor, Thomas Kimbold. He persuaded the man in charge of granting them, Robert Cooke – Clarencieux King of Arms – that the town was worthy of having one. The town's claim was probably helped by the fact that Cooke was a graduate of the university, and had granted arms to the university two years earlier. The coat of arms features a rose and a fleur-de-lis, which are royal badges and represent privileges given to the town by monarchs over the centuries. There are three ships sailing up the river under Magdalene bridge, then known as the Great Bridge, representing Cambridge's importance as a centre for river trade.

Civil War

CAMBRIDGE is one of the most attractive cities in the world today – but in Elizabethan times, it was a much less lovely place. The principal means of sanitation was the King's Ditch, which had existed since Saxon times. It was piled high with rubbish – rotting food, dung, and the entrails of animals. People had even built their own toilets, or privies, on top of it. In the 13th century, King Henry III had ordered it to be emptied, insisting that 'the town be cleansed from dirt and filth; that the watercourse should be opened and kept open as of old so that the filth may run off; and that the great ditch of the town be cleansed.' The royal edict had little impact, however. Over the years, the ditch continued to be used as an open sewer, and the town's thoroughfares were dirty too. Livestock was constantly being brought through the town to and from grazing in the surrounding fields – and butchers used the streets as a slaughterhouse.

Coupled with the dirt and the mess, Cambridge was seriously overcrowded. The growth of the university had prompted a big rise in student numbers, and an increase in the number of people servicing their needs – from cooks and servants to tailors and fencing masters. In some parishes, notably St Giles, houses were divided into tenements, and slum conditions prevailed. Needless to say, bickering between town and gown about the problem meant that nothing was done to tackle it. The town's leading citizens accused the university of causing the situation through unfettered expansion, and the academics in turn claimed the town was guilty of 'pestering every lane and corner with unwholesome cottages.'

With so much rubbish, and so much poor housing, fires were commonplace – as was the plague. The town was infested with rats, and its wells were polluted. Some of the wells were sited next to the ditch itself, and others were near graveyards.

In 1444, instead of coming to do it himself, Henry VI sent the Marquess of Suffolk to Cambridge to perform the foundation stone ceremony for King's College Chapel, because he was worried that 'the aier and the pestilence that hath long regned on our said universitie' might make him ill.

Health hazard – livestock being driven through the streets of Cambridge.

At the start of the 16th century, epidemics broke out on average every three years, spanning a 40-year period, and there were further outbreaks in the 17th century. In one of them, in 1610, the death toll reached more than 400, and in 1666, the same year as the Great Fire of London, more than 800 people died, one in eight of the town's population. The situation was so bad that plans were drawn up to establish permanent isolation hospitals for those who contracted the disease – pest houses – on Coldham's Common, but they were never built. John Evelyn, the writer and diarist of the 17th century, described Cambridge as a 'low, dirty, unpleasant place, the street ill-paved, the air thick and infected by fens.'

Some of the measures introduced to make Cambridge a cleaner, healthier place were rather bizarre by modern standards. For example, Parliament gave both the Mayor and the Vice-Chancellor, the university's top official, the power to tackle environmental nuisances, such as 'wandering hogs'. Then in 1544, a Paving Act came into force, obliging every Cambridge householder to pave the road outside his home in a bid to keep the streets cleaner. Special courts – called Paving Leets – were set up to punish people who failed to do their duty under the law.

However, in 1606, something positive was done. A group of businessmen and citizens got together with the university to see if a new water supply could be provided for the town. The idea, originally put forward more than 30 years before by Andrew Perne, the master of Peterhouse, was to bring in water from Nine Wells at Great Shelford, on the outskirts of Cambridge, in a channel that would flow into the King's Ditch, for what the university called the 'perpetual scouringe of same',

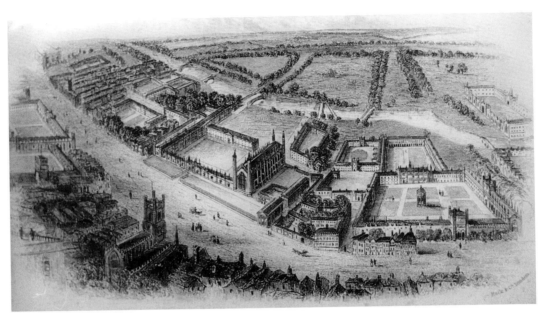

which would be 'a singular benefite for the healthsomeness both of the Universite and of the Towne.'

The key figures in this scheme were the Vice-Chancellor, Dr Stephen Perse, and Thomas Hobson, who owned stables in Cambridge and ran a horse-drawn haulage business. It is from Hobson that the well-known expression Hobson's Choice, meaning no choice at all, derives. According to legend, people going to hire a horse from him were offered the choice of any horse they wanted – provided it was the one that Hobson deemed had been rested the longest. The project was also backed by Thomas Chaplyn, lord of the manor at Trumpington, who granted the town and university a 1,000-year lease on the land on which the new watercourse would be built.

The channel was opened in 1610, and it carried fresh water from Vicar's Brook, south of the town, to a conduit in Trumpington Street – known ever since as Hobson's Conduit – all the way to a fountain in the market. By the time the water began flowing, however, part of the King's Ditch had been built over, and the conduit did not succeed in flushing it out. The main reason was felt to be the fact that the strength of the flow had been 'diluted'. Colleges along the route cut their own channels off the main one, so they could be ensured of a supply of fresh, clean water, for drinking – and for filling the master's bath. One college built a plunge pool, and another a swimming pool, both of which still exist. Today, a trust made up of local people works to maintain the ancient watercourse. At the start of the summer, the conduit is switched on, and water trickles in rivulets along its remaining runnels, which can be seen alongside the pavement in Trumpington Street.

While the fresh water helped in some degree to clean up the town, it did not eliminate the plague entirely. In the 1620s and 1630s there were several outbreaks, and Dr Henry Butts, Master of Corpus Christi College and also the Vice-Chancellor, teamed up with town officials to try to stamp it out. He believed the epidemic had effectively turned Cambridge into a disaster area, and he sent out a nationwide appeal for money to fight it. A temporary pest house was set up to nurse the victims, and taverns were closed, to prevent it spreading. Many academics, fearing for their lives, fled the town for the relative safety of the

Sidney Sussex College.

sympathisers. Many of Cambridge's historic bridges were destroyed, to prevent them being used by the enemy.

In the end, none of the elaborate preparations were necessary. The King's troops never attacked the city. The closest they got was Godmanchester, which they seized from Parliamentary troops. Cambridge feared it was next, and a student there at the time, Matthew Robinson, recorded how 'the bells rang backward and the beacons were fired as if Hannibal had been at the gates.' Cromwell sent hundreds of his troops out of the town to confront the Royalists – but the King's men refused to fight and left the area.

The confrontation showed up Cambridge's students in a pretty cowardly light. As soon as the alarm bells began to ring, they took to their heels and went into hiding in the countryside. However, Parliamentarian supporters rounded them up and forced them to come back. Cromwell then issued them with weapons – and put them on guard duty until the King's forces had departed.

Cromwell's military adroitness led to him being given command, with Sir Thomas Fairfax, of Parliament's New Model Army, the fighting force which took on and eventually defeated the Royalists in 1648, and which had its roots in the Eastern Counties Association. The following year, Charles was tried, and beheaded, in the Banqueting House at Whitehall. After Fairfax stepped down, Cromwell became sole commander of the New Model Army, and he waged successful campaigns against the Scots and the Irish, allowing England to take complete control of the British Isles for the first time in its history. He was given the title Lord Protector, and became a king-like figure himself. There is no doubt he was a great soldier, and one of the country's greatest rulers, but he was also feared, and when he died, in 1658, many people were relieved to see the back of him. Charles II came to the throne, and Royalty was back in fashion again. Two years after Cromwell's death, his body was disinterred from its resting place in Westminster Abbey, and ceremonially executed. Exactly 300 years after that in 1960, his head was buried in the ante-chapel of his old Cambridge college, Sidney Sussex.

The new King drew up a charter for Cambridge in 1685, giving him the power to appoint the Mayor, the aldermen and the other officers of the town, but during the following short and troubled reign of James II, a proclamation was issued making that charter null and void, and restoring to the Corporation its ancient rights and franchises.

David Loggan's engraving of Trinity College.

In the aftermath of the Civil War there was much bitterness in Cambridge between those who had backed Charles I, and those who had allied themselves with Parliament and Puritanism. Sometimes this bitterness was expressed violently, and groups like the Quakers, who founded the Friends' Meeting House on the corner of Jesus Lane and Park Street, faced hostility and physical retribution from some townspeople.

Near to this place was buried on 25 March 1960 the head of OLIVER CROMWELL Lord Protector of the Commonwealth of England, Scotland & Ireland, Fellow Commoner of this College 1616-7

Plaque at Sidney Sussex commemorating the burial of Cromwell's head.

Feelings ran so high, perhaps, because the town had played such a pivotal role in the war. Prof Helen Cam, in her book *A History of Cambridgeshire*, writes: 'Perhaps at no other period in its history did Cambridge exercise a more decisive influence upon national events than during the years when the regionalised forces of the Parliament were being welded into one, and Cromwell's army was being born.'

A superbly detailed picture of what life was like in Cambridge during the 17th century has been left by David Loggan, who produced engravings of both Cambridge and Oxford. His meticulous studies of the Cambridge colleges show stray dogs, burial parties, coaches, provisions arriving by river, gardens, tennis courts, and even, at Christ's, the Master's washing line. Above all, in the grandeur of the buildings portrayed, they show just how important Cambridge had become as a seat of learning.

Christ's College, depicted by Loggan.

Men of Letters, Men of Science

ALTHOUGH the Civil War will be remembered as the defining event for Cambridge in the 17th century, it was not the only important milestone in the city's history.

At the beginning of the century, Cambridge was alive with literary endeavour, and some of the most famous names in English poetry were producing their finest work. Among them, there was Andrew Marvell, who came up to Trinity College as a sizar in 1633, and whose work ranged from the erotic *To His Coy Mistress* to what is said to be the greatest political poem in English, *An Horatian Ode upon Cromwell's Return from Ireland*. There was the religious poet George Herbert, who became a Fellow of Trinity, and who was also the university's public orator for eight years from 1620. There was John Dryden, the poet, playwright and critic, yet another Trinity man. And, of course, there was the man who many rank alongside Shakespeare in the history of English literature, John Milton.

Milton came up to Christ's College in 1625, aged just 16, and quickly acquired the nickname 'The Lady of Christ's' from his fellow students, because he had, in his own words, 'a certain niceness of nature, an honest haughtiness.' His early poetry, written in Cambridge, was penned in Latin and Italian as well as in English, and includes his first great work, *On The Morning of Christ's Nativity*, written when he was only about 21. He also wrote an epitaph on Hobson, the university carrier, and despite becoming totally blind, went on to compose the finest epic poem ever written, *Paradise Lost*, using an amanuensis, or secretary, to write down the lines as he spoke them – all 11,000 of them. Today, many visitors to Christ's make a pilgrimage to the First Court, where the poet had his rooms, and to the Fellows' Garden, where the famous mulberry tree that he used to enjoy sitting under still grows.

One of Dryden's best-known poems is *The Fire of London*, which described the horrifying event of 1666 in graphic terms: 'Night came, but without darkness or repose, A dismal picture of the gen'ral doom: Where souls distracted when the Trumpet blows, And half unready when their bodies come.' Another graphic description of the great fire was written by the diarist Samuel Pepys, who was not only a Cambridge University man, but whose family also hailed from the Cambridge area. His great-grandfather had acquired a manor at Cottenham, near the city, but Pepys's father had later moved to London to seek his fortune. Pepys was born in the capital in 1633, and came to Magdalene College on a scholarship, taking his degree in 1654. Of the fire, Pepys wrote: 'We saw the fire as only one entire arch of fire from this to the other side of the bridge, and in a bow up the hill, for an arch of above a mile long. It made me weep to see it. The churches, houses, and all on fire and flaming at once, and a horrid noise the flames made, and the cracking of houses at their ruine.'

To the distress of the Puritans, known for their sombre dress, strict moral code and aversion to frivolity and fun, and to many senior members of the university, who feared for their students' virtue, Cambridge was a flourishing centre for the performance of plays, rivalling London in sophistication. It even attracted playgoers from there, many of whom made the journey on the newly-inaugurated stagecoaches, which began running between Cambridge and the capital in 1655. On their way to the theatre, however, travellers often had to endure a few unscheduled dramas en route – accidents caused by bumpy, pothole-riddled roads, and hold-ups by highwaymen.

Cambridge's literary reputation was further enhanced by its own printing house, Cambridge University Press, which published many of the major works of

the time. Among the writers associated with it were Milton, Sir Thomas Browne, the author and physician, and Richard Bentley, the great classical scholar. The Press is the oldest printing and publishing house in the world. It was founded by a royal charter granted to the university in 1534, and has been operating continuously since printing its first book in 1584. Its first printing house was built where the Senate House lawn now is, and it published the first *Cambridge Bible* in 1591.

As well as the arts, the Press served the university's scientists in the 17th century, and here, Cambridge was a world leader as well. One of the people whose work it published was William Harvey, the brilliant farmer's son whose research on the circulation of blood revolutionised medicine. After completing his

Statue of Sir Isaac Newton at Trinity College.

studies at Cambridge, Harvey went to the greatest medical school of the time, Padua, and began experiments to find out more about how blood worked in the body. He discovered that the valves of the heart, arteries and veins are one-way, and that the right ventricle of the heart supplies the lungs, and the left the rest of the arterial system. The quantity of blood pumped led him to the conclusion that 'blood must circulate'.

In 1660, Cambridge MP Henry Lucas established a chair of mathematics at the university, which was first occupied by Isaac Barrow (a classical scholar as well as a mathematician) and then by a man hailed as one of the most brilliant thinkers of all time – Isaac Newton.

Like Milton, Newton was an offbeat character, held in awe by those around him. Today, he might be called a hippy. He was a solitary man, with very long hair, and cared little about what he wore. A contemporary recalled that he often 'dined in college in stockings untied, head scarcely combed.' Born at Woolsthorpe in Lincolnshire, Newton worked in the fields of the family farm before going to Cambridge's Trinity College in 1661. Even as a schoolboy, he had shown remarkable aptitude for science, making his own water clocks and sundials, and he was only 23 when he worked out the law of gravitation – not by an apple falling on his head, as legend has it, but by observing one falling from a tree near his home. A year later, he made a discovery about light, that it can be separated by a prism,

The Pitt Building, one of Cambridge University Press's earliest buildings in the city.

The Senate House today.

and soon after, he invented the first reflecting telescope, using a parabolic mirror to magnify the object being looked at.

Newton was appointed Lucasian professor at Cambridge in 1667, but did not publish any of his work until a decade later, in a book called *Philosophiae Naturalis Principia Mathematica*. In this, he attempted to explain all physical phenomena, setting out the laws of motion, and looking at the action of the tides, and the orbits of the planets. He explained the concepts using mathematical tools he devised himself, the binomial theorem and differential calculus, now the cornerstone of modern mathematics.

He spent almost all his life in Cambridge, and for many years was President of the Royal Society, England's premier scientific institution. He was Master of the Mint too, MP for Cambridge University on two occasions, 1689-90, and 1701-2, and was knighted in 1705. The honour was conferred on him by Queen Anne during a royal visit to Cambridge, partly funded by the university, and partly by the town. Huge crowds turned out to see the event.

Einstein said of Newton that 'Nature was to him an open book, whose letters he could read without effort,' but Newton himself was more modest about his achievements. At the end of his life, in 1727, he wrote: 'I do not know what I may appear to the world, but to myself I seem to have been only like a boy playing on the seashore, and diverting myself in now and then finding a smoother pebble or a prettier shell than ordinary, whilst the great ocean of truth lay all undiscovered before me.'

The start of the 18th century saw a major plan for the redevelopment of the centre of Cambridge, drawn up by Nicholas Hawksmoor, the architect who worked closely with Sir Christopher Wren. Hawksmoor's scheme involved knocking down a number of buildings, creating a covered market, and building a new university church. The plan foundered, but instead, the university embarked on improvements to the Schools area, including the construction of the Senate House, where the General Admission to Degrees ceremony is held. Work on the classically-inspired building, with its Corinthian columns and pilasters, started in about 1722, and was finished by 1730.

Wren himself was responsible for some of Cambridge's most beautiful buildings. In 1663, aged 31, he had designed Pembroke College's chapel, and over a 14-year period from 1676 had created the library at Trinity College, aided by England's greatest craftsman of the time, Grinling Gibbons, who adorned the bookcases with exquisitely carved fruit and flowers.

Hawksmoor's radical revamp of the city centre was not the only grandiose plan for the university. In the 1770s, St John's College hired Capability Brown to design

Dons gather in the Senate House.

a garden for its Fellows, and while he was working on it, he came up with a proposal to landscape the Backs, and create a huge park that would serve all the colleges there.

Not long before this, in 1762, Richard Walker, the Vice-Master of Trinity College, had presented the university with five acres of land near Free School Lane, 'for the purpose of a public Botanic Garden'. He had bought the land a couple of years before, and the aim was to further the cause of medicine by carrying out experiments to see whether any new plant-based treatments could be discovered. At the time, there was great interest in science, and the university had begun to make its first academic appointments in fields like chemistry, so Walker saw the garden purely as a laboratory, declaring that 'flowers and fruits must be looked

Trinity College library, designed by Wren.

The Botanic Garden.

upon as amusement only.' What he did not know at the time was that the soil on the chosen site was poor, and not very suitable for growing trials. The site also proved too small. In 1831, however, another location was to be found, where the Botanic Garden is now, and planting began there soon after.

Relations between town and gown continued to be fragile, especially on the vexed issue of public entertainment. In 1701, the Corporation had agreed to the staging of a series of plays at Sturbridge Fair, but the university was opposed to the idea, and mustered an ad-hoc army of dons, more than 60 of them, to go to the common and insist that the stage be taken down. Later, university pressure led to the passing of the Players and Tavern Act, which decreed that anyone trying to put on a play in Cambridge or Oxford would be deemed a rogue and a vagabond, and could be kicked out of town.

The academics' misgivings about the propriety of such events had been grimly justified by a tragic event, ten years before the passing of the act. More than 80 people died when fire swept through a makeshift theatre at Barnwell. A play was being put on in a barn with a thatched roof, and a candle triggered a blaze in the hayloft. Many of those who lost their lives were burned to death, and others were trampled trying to escape.

Fire almost deprived the nation of one of its finest poets too. Thomas Gray, best known for his *Elegy Written in a Country Churchyard*, was a Fellow-commoner at Peterhouse from 1742, and his rooms were on the top floor. He was worried about how he might escape if a fire broke out, so he had irons attached to the outer wall so he could climb down to safety if need be. A group of undergraduates at the college decided to see if the fire escape would work, and set Gray's rooms alight. Choking from the smoke, the poet did manage to get out, but he subsequently switched colleges, moving to Pembroke.

Cambridge was also home in the late 18th century to two other major literary figures, William Wordsworth and Samuel Taylor Coleridge. Wordsworth was a student at St John's College, and Coleridge was at Jesus, and the two collaborated on several projects. A selection of their work, *Lyrical Ballads*, was published in 1798, ushering in the age of Romanticism in English poetry, and it was at Wordsworth's suggestion that Coleridge, a brilliant classical scholar while at Cambridge, wrote one of his most famous poems, *The Rime of the Ancient Mariner.*

Although Wordsworth did not enjoy the academic life in Cambridge, and soon quit the town for France to experience the excitement of the revolution there, he retained an affection for it. When Cambridge finally got gas lighting, in 1823, the poet travelled all the way from his Lake District home to admire the effect.

One of England's greatest statesmen, William Pitt, was also at Cambridge in the mid-18th century. He became Prime Minister at the age of 24, and safely steered the country through 17 years of troubled times, including the French wars.

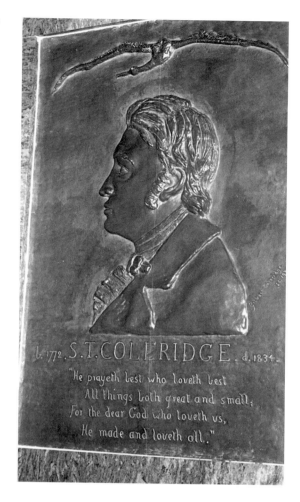

Memorial to Samuel Taylor Coleridge at Jesus College.

The university saw little major change in the 18th century, but it was a different story for the town. After centuries of being an unhealthy, rather parochial place with few facilities, it finally got decent roads, new shops, its own newspapers, and a proper hospital.

The better roads came about due to a body called the Improvement Commissioners. Originally, they were called the Paving Commissioners, and they were set up to make sure that Cambridge was cleaned up, properly paved, and had street lighting. The new organisation swiftly achieved the lighting, with the first lamps installed the same year it was founded, in 1788. The first street, Petty Cury, was paved that year too, with the rest of the town centre completed by 1793.

The roads between Cambridge and other parts of the country were improved as well, thanks to a series of Acts of Parliament passed between 1724 and 1797. At the start of the 18th century, coach travel was a luxury enjoyed only by the well-off, and it was a slow way to go. Getting to London from Cambridge by coach took about 15 hours. By the second half of the century, however, the journey time had been cut dramatically, and there was a daily service between the town and the capital. In the early years of the following century, 10 coaches were leaving Cambridge every weekday for a range of destinations, two of them for Oxford. The increase in road travel prompted an explosion in the number of coaching inns in Cambridge. Some, like The Eagle in Bene't Street, became the regular setting-off

William Pitt's statue at Pembroke College.

PITT

points for the daily services. Another was the White Horse Inn at the bottom of Castle Street, which now houses the Cambridge & County Folk Museum. Coaches would pull in, and while their passengers had a meal and freshened up, the horses would be fed and changed. Sometimes an overnight stay would be necessary. The passengers occupied the bedrooms upstairs, and the coachmen would sleep downstairs near the bar on wooden benches, made with special cupboards underneath so the day's takings could be kept close at hand and safe from thieves.

The rising number of inns helped to provide better amenities for townsfolk. As well as being a place to drink and socialise, many doubled as theatres and even concert venues. The Black Bear, for example, the yard of which survives today as Market Passage, was the meeting place for Cambridge's Music Club, and staged performances of works by Handel, Purcell, and the other major composers of the day.

More frequent coaches also gave a boost to the mail. It was now possible to write to someone in London, and receive a reply the following day.

Cambridge's river, the Cam, for centuries the main highway to the town, continued to be important for transporting goods, and there were even proposals to link it with the Thames by canal, via the River Stort – but its days as a major thoroughfare were numbered. By the middle of the next century, the railway would have reached Cambridge, providing a new, and much quicker method of moving freight.

In the late 18th century, commerce and shopping began to take off in the town. Cambridge's first bank was opened in 1780 by John Mortlock, a businessman who also owned a considerable amount of land in the area, and who was to become Mayor of Cambridge 13 times, as well as an MP for the town. Cambridge also had a department store by the end of the century, the shop that was to become Eaden Lilley. Originally a haberdashery, the store went through a series of ownership changes in the 1780s and 1790s, with Thomas Hovell emerging as proprietor in

Victorian Times

BY the start of the 19th century, the population of Cambridge was close to 10,000, double what it had been 300 years before – and by the end of the century it had more than doubled again. The centre of the city was characterised by narrow streets, crammed with houses, and fields outside the town to the south and east, freed for development under the Enclosure Acts of 1801 and 1807, were used to build more new homes.

The conversion of the open fields was unpopular with some people, especially cottagers who suddenly found themselves dispossessed of the land they had been occupying for many years. The result of it all, however, was to make farming more efficient, and help the expansion of the town, which desperately needed room to grow.

In some parts of Cambridge, housing conditions were dreadful. Sanitation was non-existent. There were no toilets or public baths, and some people had to walk a quarter of a mile to get clean water. The River Cam had become an open sewer, and one report described the way some people were living as 'so wretched as to be a disgrace to civilisation'. For four months at the beginning of 1815, there was a serious outbreak of typhoid, reminiscent of the years when Cambridge was being hit by frequent bouts of the plague.

By rights, the crisis ought to have been tackled by the body with the power to improve things, the Corporation, but it failed to do so. Although there were nearly 160 aldermen, many of them lived outside the city, and they showed little interest in Cambridge's problems. Others were openly corrupt, using their influence to engineer land deals that brought them enormous profits, and buying each other 'gifts' with money from the public purse. Such abuses were not unique to Cambridge, and a commission was set up nationally to investigate a large number of towns and cities. One of the places it examined was Cambridge, and when it produced its report, the commission made no bones about accusing the Corporation of 'shameless profligacy' and 'inveterate dishonesty'.

By the mid-1830s, reform of the municipal system was under way, and

Queen Victoria's wedding to Prince Albert of Saxe-Coburg, 1840.

The Fitzwilliam Museum.

democracy at last made an appearance. The number of aldermen was reduced, and a new, elected council was set up, with 30 councillors covering five wards.

Two other major events set the city on a more progressive path at this time. The first was the beginning of Queen Victoria's reign, in 1837.

The new Queen and her husband, Prince Albert of Saxe-Coburg, were devout believers in family life – they had nine children – and they wanted to do something

to help ease the poverty that many people were forced to endure. Industry and trade, they felt, were the way forward, and they tried to encourage new ideas in a bid to make the nation a more prosperous place for all. In the early 1850s, for example, Albert was the driving force behind the Great Exhibition, a vast showcase for British invention and ingenuity that astonished the world.

The Prince Consort was also a major reforming force for Cambridge University. In 1847, he became the university's Chancellor, and very quickly came to realise that the institution was not being run as it should. In science, for example, Cambridge's teaching and research work lagged behind most of the other top educational establishments in Europe. There were other anomalies too, such as the lack of an entrance examination for students. This effectively allowed the university to ensure places for young men from the 'right sort' of families, namely the aristocracy, while excluding those it deemed unsuitable, however bright they were. Student numbers were small – in 1849, there were just over 1,700 doing courses.

The Fitzwilliam Museum's grand staircases.

With Albert's support, a Royal Commission was set up in 1850 to look into the future not only of Cambridge University, but also of Oxford and Dublin. The aim was to 'assist in the adaptation of those important institutions to the requirements of modern times.' Cambridge's dons felt the commission was an unwarranted intrusion in the running of the university, and mounted a petition against it, but it went ahead anyway. The commission recommended that new subjects should be introduced, such as engineering, as well as new professorships and lectureships, and it said the Government should pay for the cost of facilities such as laboratories, with the university paying the extra wages involved.

The Prince Consort's installation as Chancellor took place during a visit by himself and the Queen to Cambridge. On the big day, in July 1847, every shop in the town closed at 10am, and almost everyone turned out to watch the royal couple being driven to Trinity College with a cavalry escort. With them was a great English hero of the time, the man who had conquered Napoleon at Waterloo, the Duke of Wellington. During the day, the royals attended a Grand Horticultural Fete at Cambridge's newest college, Downing, and a dinner at Trinity, where the guests included the Cambridge astronomer John Couch Adams, and Urbain Leverrier, the French astronomer, both of whom had been credited with discovering a new planet, Neptune.

While the Queen and Prince Albert were in Cambridge, they also went to see how work was going on a building that was to be one of the university's most impressive achievements of the 19th century. The Fitzwilliam Museum had been launched as an idea three decades before, in 1816 – only a few months after Wellington's victory at Waterloo, in fact – thanks to a bequest by Richard, 7th Viscount Fitzwilliam. Work was now under way on building it in Trumpington Street, on land bought from Peterhouse. It was a magnificent building, in a classical

Interior of the Fitzwilliam Museum in the 1840s, by Ebeneezer Challis.

Right and below: Coronation fete, Midsummer Common.

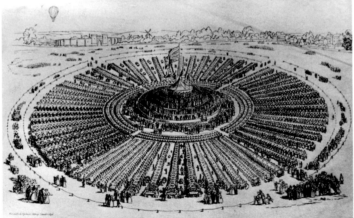

style unlike most other buildings in Cambridge. Fitzwilliam wanted it to be a living classroom for the university's students, a place where they could see and learn about great works of art, as well as architecture and archaeology. Among his bequests were medieval illuminated manuscripts, paintings by Titian and Veronese, and the finest collection of Rembrandt etchings in England. Work on the museum – whose entrance was guarded by a pair of stone lions which legend says come to life at night and stalk Cambridge's streets – finished in 1875. Over the years, other bequests, donations and purchases, such as works by Van Dyck, Gainsborough, and Monet, have turned the museum's collection of art into one of the best in Europe, and perhaps the world. It also has Egyptian, Greek and Roman antiquities, and a big collection of Chinese porcelain.

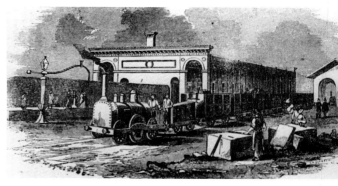

Wood engraving of Cambridge railway station, 1845.

The huge crowds who turned out to see the royal couple on their visit to Cambridge are an indication of how popular Queen Victoria was, and had been ever since her coronation. On that day, in June 1838, Cambridge had thrown its biggest-ever party – a feast for 15,000 people on Midsummer Common. The revellers munched their way through more than 7,000 joints of

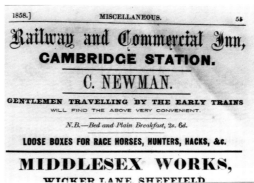

Advertisement for accommodation near the station, 1858.

Trade on the River Cam was dealt a fatal blow by the railways.

beef, mutton, pork, veal and bacon, 72 lb of mustard, 144 lb of salt, 125 gallons of pickles, and 4,500 loaves. For dessert, there were 1,600 plum puddings, made with 10 sacks of flour, 2,400 lb of raisins, 825 lb of suet, 360 gallons of milk, and 3,300 eggs. The enormous meal was washed down with nearly 100 barrels of ale. Three circles of tables seated 2,762 children, and 60 more catered for 12,720 adults. Serving them were 351 stewards, 547 carvers, 441 waiters, and 297 beer waiters. Afterwards, for those not too bloated by food and drink, there were sports, and then a firework display.

As well as the coronation of Queen Victoria, the other event of major significance for Cambridge in the 19th century was the coming of the railway.

The town's station, on the London to Norwich route operated by Great Eastern, was opened in 1845, and within a few years, other lines linking Cambridge with big towns in the region were up and running as well. Six companies ran trains in and out of the station, and they would have liked it to be sited right in the centre of town, but there was fierce opposition from shopkeepers, and from the university and colleges. The university maintained that the noise from the locomotives would shatter the studious atmosphere of Cambridge's libraries, college courts and exam rooms, and it eventually got its way. The station was built a mile from the centre, and even the tracks themselves were curved in an arc to keep them well away from the town. The university won the right to impose fines on the train companies, too, if they infringed its peace and quiet.

The railways led to an employment boom for Cambridge. There was already a large and growing workforce involved in the brewery trade, flour-milling and printing, and now, coal yards had to be built to keep the trains fuelled, and that meant more jobs. More workers meant more houses, so brick and tile works were built at Cherry Hinton and in Coldham's Lane, and a cement works was opened at Romsey Town, where many of Cambridge's new homes were being constructed.

However, the trains signalled the death knell for the river trade that had sustained Cambridge's economy for centuries. As people switched to rail freight, fewer and fewer barges made the journey from King's Lynn to the Cambridge hythes. A century before, in an article in *The Foreigner's Companion*, the importance of the river traffic in keeping Cambridge people fed, and warm, was spelled out in no uncertain terms: 'The purest wine they receive by the way of Lynn: flesh, fish, wild-fowl, poultry, butter, cheese, and all manner of provisions, from the adjacent country. Living is cheap: coals from seven pence to nine pence a bushel; turf, or rather peat, four shillings a thousand; sedge, with which the bakers heat their ovens, four shillings per hundred sheaves. These, together with osiers, reeds and rushes used in several trades, are daily imported by the River Cam. Great quantities of oil, made from flax seed, cole seed, hemp and other seeds, ground or pressed by the numerous mills in the Isle of Ely, are brought up by this river also. By this river they also receive 1,500 or 2,000 firkins of butter every week, which is sent by waggon to London.'

The river was also the lifeblood of Sturbridge Fair, but by the time the trains came, the fair too was on its last legs. Once more than a month long, it lasted for three just days in 1897, and had dwindled from a fairground the size of a small town to a few alleys of amusements and confectionery stalls. The coach business,

*Town Bumps in the
1880s.*

*College rowing crews
gave the river a new
lease of life.*

and many of the inns which served it in Cambridge, also came to the end of the
road, although the Cambridge to Bedford stage carried on until 1894.

The river got a new lease of life, however, thanks to the colleges, which took
advantage of the drop in commercial traffic to launch their own boat clubs. Within
a few years, the clubs were competing in an annual race, now called the May
Bumps, in which crews had to try to catch the boat in front, and bump its stern. As
with many college sporting events, things could sometimes get out of hand, and
after an accident in which a rower was hit by the prow of a boat and killed, the rules
were changed so that contact between boats was not necessary for a 'bump' to be
registered. The coxswain of the boat being pursued simply had to raise his hand if
his boat was overtaken. Later, in the 1880s, town boat races were launched as well.

*The original
Cavendish Laboratory.*

Downing College.

In 1829, the first ever Boat Race between Oxford and Cambridge was rowed, at Henley-on-Thames. The Oxford crew wore straw hats with broad blue ribbons, jerseys with large dark blue stripes, and canvas trousers, and their Cambridge rivals wore white, with dapper pink neckties. Although the race had never been staged before, it aroused enormous interest, because of the established academic rivalry between the two towns. Two years before, the first inter-varsity cricket match had also been held, and more than 20,000 people crammed the banks of the two-and-a-half mile river course at Henley for the Boat Race. Newspapers were packed with

The Bridge of Sighs, built by St John's College in 1832.

pre-race and post-race reports – Oxford emerged the victors – and the authorities at Henley allowed a fair to be held, with fireworks. Inspired by the race's success, and delighted by the trade it brought, they launched an event of their own a few years later, which was to become equally famous – Henley Regatta.

The second Boat Race did not take place until 1836, and on that occasion, it was held on a five and three-quarter-mile course between Westminster and Putney. Cambridge got their revenge for their defeat in the inaugural race, winning by almost a minute.

One of the cheering spectators at that very first race in 1829 was a young Cambridge student destined to become one of the most famous scientists of all time – Charles Darwin. He was fascinated by botany and geology,

Bust of Charles Darwin, Christ's College.

"STRINGENT MEASURES!"

Topical Series—Published by the Cambridge Picture Post Card Co.

Mr Aberdein's Papyruseum exhibition.

and his professor at Cambridge, John Stevens Henslow – the man who helped to acquire the Botanic Garden's current site – encouraged him to start collecting and cataloguing beetles. It was Henslow who gave Darwin a reference for the job of naturalist aboard HMS *Beagle*, the survey ship that set off on a voyage around the world in 1831 to study flora, fauna and geological formations. The trip took five years to complete, but it was not until nearly three decades later that Darwin – who had once ironically considered a career as a vicar – published the book that was to bring the fury of the clergy raining down on his head, *On The Origin of Species By Means of Natural Selection*. His observations in South America and Australia had convinced Darwin that the popular theory about man and animals, that they had always been as they were, was wrong. The truth, Darwin was convinced, was that they had gradually evolved from earlier, simpler species that had originally been single-cell creatures. Natural selection was the process by which some species changed to survive – survival of the fittest. The church saw the book as an attack on the Biblical story of the Creation, but Darwin's ideas were largely accepted within a few years of being published.

Another great scientist in the early years of the century was Charles Babbage. A brilliant, self-taught mathematician, his knowledge was more extensive than that of his tutors when he arrived at Trinity College in 1814, and he went on to follow in the footsteps of Isaac Newton by becoming Lucasian Professor. As a student, he would even translate

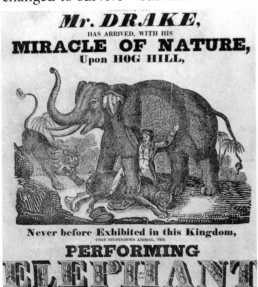

Handbill advertising the arrival of Mr Drake's elephant.

foreign textbooks into English so his tutors could use them in classes. Babbage believed the mathematical tables being used at the time were inaccurate, and he set himself the task of inventing a machine that would give error-free results. In 1822, he produced his Difference Engine Number 1, which used toothed wheels to perform calculations. It worked on decimal principles, and was the forerunner of the machine that nearly everyone now uses – the computer.

Science really took off at Cambridge University in the 19th century. Its great champion was William Whewell, Master of Trinity, an omnipresent figure in all the main scientific movements of the early 1800s. He was Professor of Mineralogy, and also did pioneering research into the light-refracting properties of crystals. He even collected tide data, so that tide timetables could be created – and it was he who coined the word 'scientist'.

Newnham College's first students.

In 1870, the Cavendish Laboratory was built, thanks to an endowment by the Duke of Devonshire. It was there that some of the most important early discoveries of physics were made. The lab's first professor, James Clerk Maxwell, there between 1871 and 1879, made ground-breaking studies of electricity and magnetism; the second, Lord Rayleigh (1879-84), led early research into radiation; and his successor, J.J. Thomson, in charge between 1885 and 1919, was the man who discovered the electron, laying the foundations for electronics and the computer technology we take for granted today.

As well as the Cavendish, labs and museums sprang up on the New Museums Site and the Downing Site, and to the west of the city, the university's observatory, which had been built in 1822, was expanded with extra buildings. Subjects for teaching and research multiplied and facilities improved, as did the quality of teaching, and methods of examination.

Work on Downing College had begun in 1807, using money left in the will of Sir George Downing, whose grandfather gave his name to London's Downing Street. Sir George had died more than half a century before, in 1749, and had stipulated

Girton College ladies fire brigade, 1887.

that should various relatives die childless, his estates should be used to found a new Cambridge college. The architect, William Wilkins, opted for a classical Greek style, and though his original plans could not be finished for lack of funds, his successors stuck to his initial idea.

Existing colleges continued to grow, and many added new buildings, and in some cases, startling architectural features. In 1832, for example, St John's built its own version of Venice's Bridge of Sighs – today one of the city's most photographed tourist attractions.

Many colleges also discovered a spirit of commercial enterprise in the 1870s and 1880s, and began to develop land they owned in and around the centre of Cambridge, not with academic buildings, but with houses, for their Fellows and for the university's burgeoning army of staff. In 1882, college Fellows were freed from the restriction that they must resign their Fellowship if they married, and many wasted no time in tying the knot. The need to accommodate them, their new wives, and their children, led to the boom in terraced housing that now characterises the east and north sides of Cambridge.

As it moved toward the 20th century, the university finally ditched many of its outmoded practices. Its supervision of weights and measures, and of markets and fairs, was abolished. Public houses no longer had to be licensed by the Vice-Chancellor, and he also relinquished his right to license theatrical performances. This was good news for theatres like the Barnwell Theatre Royal, which was immensely popular – Charles Dickens gave readings of his books there – and the

Selwyn College.

New Theatre, in St Andrew's Street, built on the site of the former St Andrew's Hall. Travelling exhibitions were also a big attraction, like the Papyruseum, a strange collection of historical models that went on show at the Black Bear inn, and Mr Drake's Performing Elephant, which drew big crowds.

There was one aspect of modern times that the university refused to embrace – the admission of women. Demands that the all-male bastion should open its doors to women began in the middle of the 19th century with a request that girls should be able to sit the university's local examinations. At first, the university said no, with the concession that examiners could mark, in a private capacity, any papers submitted from girls' schools. However, protesters launched a petition, and eventually the dons were obliged to give in. The next step was the establishment of separate colleges for women. In 1869, the first five women students were admitted to a tiny educational establishment called Benslow House, at Hitchin, and four years later, the fledgling college moved to Cambridge – to a site on the edge of the town at Girton, to keep its young ladies safe from the attentions of the male students. In 1871, a second women's college was founded, Newnham, at first consisting only of five students and a tutor based in a house in Regent Street, but later moving to its modern-day home in Sidgwick Avenue.

Eventually, women were allowed to attend lectures, although there was precious little recognition of their presence. Many male academics still began their lectures with the salutation 'Gentlemen,...' Women were also allowed to work alongside men in the university's laboratories, but their right to become members of the university by taking degrees was still a long way off. Attempts were made in 1887 and 1897 to admit them to full membership, but both failed – and it was to be half a century before they finally won that battle.

Another new male college appeared before the century was out, Selwyn, founded in 1882 by the Bishop of Lichfield with the aim of encouraging students to enter the Church of England ministry.

The Leys School.

Several great names lit up the university in the early years of the century. Lord Byron arrived in 1805, as a student at Trinity College. He was not the most dedicated of undergraduates, spending much of his time rehearsing the dissolute life he was later to lead in England and abroad. He enjoyed boxing and other sports, and had a small bear for a pet, which he led about the college on a chain.

Lord Byron.

Of his tutor, the poet wrote: 'Unlucky Tavell! Doomed to daily cares by pugilistic pupils and by bears.'

Alfred Tennyson was a Trinity student in the 1820s, and was awarded a special medal by the Chancellor in 1829 for his poem *Timbuctoo*. Twenty years later, he published *In Memoriam*, said by many to be his finest poem, an elegy mourning the death of his friend Arthur Hallam, also a Trinity man. That same year, he succeeded Wordsworth as Poet Laureate.

Charles Kingsley, author of *The Water Babies*, was at Magdalene in the 1830s, and returned in 1860 as Professor of Modern History. One of his students was Edward, Prince of Wales, later to become Edward VII. Charles Babbington Macaulay, author of the History of England was another graduate of Trinity, and it was there, towards the end of the century, that Lytton Strachey, Leonard Woolf and

Thoby Stephen first met and formed the nucleus of what was later to be the Bloomsbury Group, the group of artists, writers and intellectuals whose members were also to include the novelists E.M. Forster, and Woolf's wife Virginia.

Another of the university's most famous sons was Viscount Palmerston, who was elected as Cambridge's MP in 1806, three years after entering St John's College. He served two terms as Prime Minister, the first of which saw him leading the nation in the Crimean War against Russia in 1855.

As the university expanded and improved its facilities, so things got better for the town. There were improvements in schools, the first lending library, more shops, a new water supply, a new newspaper – and a new bridge.

Since the start of the 18th century, the education of the town's children had been largely provided by the Schools, a group of establishments that were open and free to all poor children in the borough. These were founded by William Whiston, Lucasian Professor of Mathematics in 1704, and later became known as the Old Schools. In the 19th century, two other kinds of school came on the scene. One was started by the education pioneer Joseph Lancaster, and was run on Quaker principles. It began life in the Friends' Meeting House, and then moved to a new building on Pound Hill. The other new schools were the Bell Schools, or National Schools, promoted by the National Society for the Propagation of Christian Knowledge. Several of these were opened, and they provided good, basic teaching for youngsters until the coming of the first council schools, established under the Education Act of 1902. The principal public secondary school in Cambridge, and the only one until the 20th century, was the Perse School. This had been founded as far back as 1615, when Stephen Perse, a Gonville and Caius Fellow who had

become rich from a career in medicine, left some money in his will for it to be established. It provided education for about 100 boys, and was originally in Free School Lane, moving to its modern-day home in Hills Road in 1890. Cambridge also had The Leys school, a Methodist-run, boys-only school founded in 1875.

In 1855, the Town Library was opened. It was located in the Friends' Meeting House, which at that time was unoccupied, and its first librarian was John Pink. He was passionate about the heritage of Cambridge, and he built up a big collection of local history books as well as reference books, many of which are still there today in the Cambridgeshire Collection, the archive at the Central Library in

Tennyson's statue at Trinity College.

TENNYSON

AUGUST 6. 1809

Joshua Taylor's store.

Lion Yard. Readers had tickets, as they do today, but they were not allowed to browse among the shelves. They had to look through a catalogue at the front counter, choose the book they wanted, and an assistant would then go to get it for them. It was not until the 1920s that open access, giving people the chance to wander among the shelves, was allowed.

More shops began to appear in the town centre, among them Joshua Taylor, the outfitters, which got started in 1810, expanding into its Market Street premises in 1900. Another was Robert Sayle. Its eponymous founder was the son of a rich Norfolk sheep farmer, who gave the young man the princely sum of £500 to start his own business. Young Robert rented a shop in St Andrew's Street in 1840, at first selling only linen, drapery, hosiery and haberdashery, but as time went on, carpets, furs and household goods were added.

The voracious appetite of students and dons for the printed word led to the

Robert Sayle – an early advertisement.

founding of Heffers bookshop in 1876. It began as a small stationery shop in Fitzroy Street, but by the turn of the century had broken the monopoly of the London booksellers in Cambridge, and had become the only local shop to supply textbooks to the university. It later branched out into children's books and printing.

Agriculture was still very important

in the 19th century, and the town had a hay market, a cattle market, and a corn exchange, set up in Downing Street in 1842. In 1885 the cattle market was permanently located on its present site off Hills Road, although it is no longer used for that purpose.

The development of the town centre was plunged into chaos in 1849, when a huge fire swept through it. The blaze broke out just after midnight on September 15, a Saturday night, and no one ever found out how it started, but it caused enormous damage to the market area. Nearly a dozen fire engines, some of them the colleges' own brigades, rushed to the scene, but the keys to open and turn on Hobson's Conduit, then sited in the

Robert Sayle – the founder.

Heffers book shop.

place, were missing. Water had to brought by bucket, in a human chain, from the river. Shopkeepers and stallholders threw their stock through doors and windows onto the street, as the flames spread from building to building. One shop, a chemist's, was at risk of a gas explosion, but the police managed to reach the gasworks in time to turn off the supply. The fire lasted for nearly six hours, and by the time it was under control on Sunday morning, eight buildings had been completely destroyed.

Although people were devastated by the blaze at the time, it proved to be a blessing in disguise. The market had been getting more and more overcrowded, and a major revamp had been necessary for a while. The fire cleared away a number of buildings, and the rest were later demolished, allowing the present four-sided market area to be created.

In 1888, Cambridge's first daily newspaper hit the streets – the *Cambridge Daily News*. The paper was the brainchild of a man not from Cambridge, but from Bury St Edmunds, William Farrow Taylor. At first it was only four pages in size, each of five columns, and there were no pictures. Journalists had to write out their copy by hand, and then compositors would set it in type, a single piece of type being used for each individual letter. It was then printed on a flat-bed press, with the paper being fed in by hand, sheet by sheet. A sister paper, the *Cambridge Weekly News*, was founded about the same time, and that later absorbed its rival, the *Independent Press*.

The *Daily News*, like its modern-day descendant the *Evening News*, prided itself on championing the causes of its readers, and after a public outcry about the drinking booths that had become commonplace at the annual Midsummer Fair,

Front page of the Cambridge Daily News first edition, in 1888.

the paper succeeded in getting them removed. It was also instrumental in ridding Cambridge of one of its most hated institutions – the Spinning House. This was originally a workhouse, set up in 1628 by Thomas Hobson, the carrier, with the altruistic aim of providing decent work for the unemployed, who could eke out a living there making garments and doing sewing jobs. By the 19th century, however, it had become a women's prison. Cambridge had its own gaol nearby, opened in 1827 in Gonville Place overlooking Parker's Piece, but that was pulled down in 1878. The Spinning House served as a place of detention not for hardened criminals, but for petty crooks and vagabonds – and women suspected of being prostitutes. The university was anxious that its young male students should not fall prey to the Oldest Profession, and its officials took to rounding up women they suspected of being 'on the game', and sending them to the Spinning House. There

they were flogged, usually by the Town Crier, who was paid a shilling a head. It was summary justice of the worst sort, guaranteed to lead to many innocent young women being imprisoned unfairly. A visitor to the Spinning House in 1776 was appalled at the conditions he found. Some of the women had been there for up to six months, he reported, trying to survive on the pennies they were paid for spinning or beating hemp. The building had no heating, and there were no beds – the inmates had to sleep on straw. Equally outraged that such a medieval institution should still be in existence in 'modern' Cambridge, the *Daily News* mounted a vigorous campaign to get it shut down, and it was duly closed at the end of the century. A new police station for Cambridge was built on the site.

The demand for new homes and more shops also saw Mill Road developed, and in Chesterton, a large area of land called the De Freville Estate came on the market, and many houses were built there. The growth of that district soon prompted the need for a direct route to it, and the most obvious line was across Midsummer Common. There was opposition to the idea, but the advocates of progress won the day, and Victoria Bridge was built, in 1890.

Soon after, a fresh water supply was found for the town, from Cherry Hinton, and at about the same time, the Cambridge University and Town Water Company was formed. By 1895, a system of deep sewers had been built, with a pumping station two miles from the town centre, and Cambridge at last managed to cast off its long-standing reputation for being one of the smelliest places in East Anglia. Until the sewerage system was built, raw sewage from homes and businesses poured straight into the river between Magdalene Bridge and Barnwell Pool. There were nearly 20 outfalls, making the Cam a cesspool. A correspondent in the newspaper, in 1888, wrote: 'It seems a wonder that more boating men are not laid up with typhoid fever.'

One other big innovation in Cambridge as the century came to a close was a form of transport for which the city is now known the length and breadth of Britain – the bicycle. The early machines were like hobby-horses, with two wheels connected by a wooden beam. By the 1880s, however, wire wheels, metal frames,

A cycling club gets set to pedal off.

and solid rubber tyres had appeared, and bizarre bikes like the Penny Farthing could be seen on the streets. In 1888 came the chain-drive 'safety' bicycle, equipped with pneumatic tyres.

Soon, cyclists were competing for road space with trams – the Cambridge Street Tramways Company was formed in 1878, and lines were laid from the railway station to Christ's College, and to Senate House Hill, via Lensfield Road and Trumpington Street. There were two open-top double-deckers, and four saloons, and they were not the quickest form of transport – walking was just as quick. Nevertheless, like bikes, trains, new shops, and all the other developments Cambridge was seeing, they were a potent image of a new era – the 20th century.

The New Century

A T THE start of the 1900s, Queen Victoria had been on the throne for more than 60 years – but she did not to see much of the wonderful new century her long reign had paved the way for, and which had begun in such a blaze of hope. On 22 January 1901, it was announced the Queen was dead, and that her son Edward, the Prince of Wales, was king.

The *Cambridge Daily News* reported: 'A feeling of profound sympathy had prevailed throughout the royal patient's illness, and when at length the death announcement arrived, there was universal sorrow and gloom. Royal Standards are flying half-mast, and black ties and other emblems of mourning are being worn by members of the University and the townsmen. Blinds are drawn in numberless cases, and black shutters appear at the windows of almost all business establishments.

'As soon as the painful intelligence was received, it was conveyed to the New Theatre, where a large number of people had already assembled in anticipation of the night's performance. The news was received by the audience in silence, and then the announcement was made that the performance would not take place.'

DEATH OF
Queen Victoria.

HER MAJESTY SINKS SLOWLY TO REST

SCENE AT THE BEDSIDE.

THE WORLD IN MOURNING.

How the Daily News *reported the death of Queen Victoria.*

Next page: Busy town centre – Petty Curry and Market Hill.

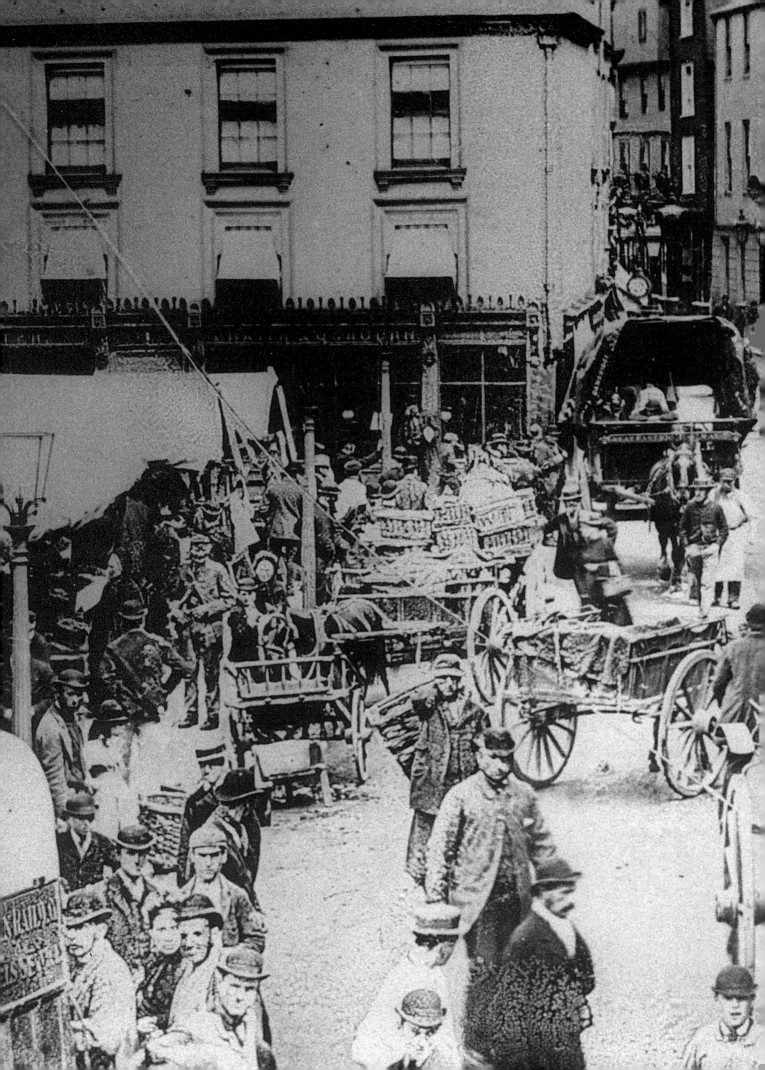

University Arms Hotel – roaring trade.

The University Arms Hotel, Cambridge.

Excellent Stabling AND Carriages.

Close to the Colleges. — * — Electric Light.

New Wing, in course of erection, including New Dining Hall, will be opened in August, 1900.

FIRST-CLASS FAMILY HOTEL. M. D. BRADFORD,
UNRIVALLED POSITION. *Proprietor.*

Like Victoria, Edward VII was linked to Cambridge, having spent a term at the university, and although he was known for his wayward behaviour – he had been cited in two divorce cases – he turned out to be a very effective and popular monarch. Huge crowds gathered to hear the proclamation that he was King. In Cambridge, the announcement was made in the Senate House, and then repeated

Chivers jam factory.

Inside Eaden Lilley.

outside next to the University Registrary. Then the proclamation was made again the next day, by both the Mayor and the High Sheriff, at different locations.

Before 1900, Cambridge was very much a university town, but in the first two decades of the 20th century, it became something more – a thriving shopping centre for East Anglia, and the cradle for what were to be the region's biggest and most successful businesses.

The University Arms Hotel in the town centre was doing a roaring trade as the new century dawned, so much so that it built a new wing in 1900. On the edge of the town, at Histon, Chivers was making a national name for itself with its jellies and jams. The Co-op was expanding rapidly in the Cambridge area, and by 1900, when it opened a big new shop in Burleigh Street, it already had several branches in the town. As well as Joshua Taylor, Eaden Lilley and Robert Sayle, there was another big department store, Matthew & Son, a grocer's shop, Hallack & Bond, the Belfast Linen Warehouse, which opened in 1905, and Laurie & McConnal Universal Stores, which was completely destroyed by fire in 1903, but then rebuilt. The town was also a major centre for brewing. There were several commercial breweries, and the university itself was even involved in the trade, making its own brew, Audit Ale, so named because university tenants were given a glass of it after settling their rents.

Cambridge also began to carve out a reputation as a centre for engineering. In 1909, an enterprising young man, David Marshall, who had begun his working life as a humble apprentice in the kitchens of Trinity College, founded a business that has

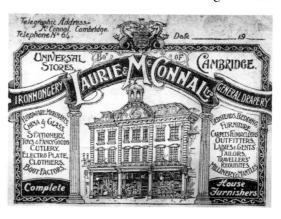

Destroyed by fire then rebuilt: Laurie & McConnal.

MILLINERY

SHOW ROOM

LADIES

W EADEN LILLEY & Cº LIMITED 12

A Metallurgique outside Marshall's first garage.

The airship that fascinated Arthur Marshall, taking off after being repaired.

since grown to become Cambridge's biggest private employer, the automobile and aerospace company that bears his name. Marshall started off running a chauffeur service for wealthy dons and students, using cars he kept in a stable in Brunswick Gardens, and within three years had opened up proper garage premises in Jesus Lane. That same year, fate opened the door to what was to become another major Marshall business. A stricken Army airship was forced to make an emergency landing near the Jesus Lane garage,

David Marshall.

Previous page: Eaden Lilley's store.

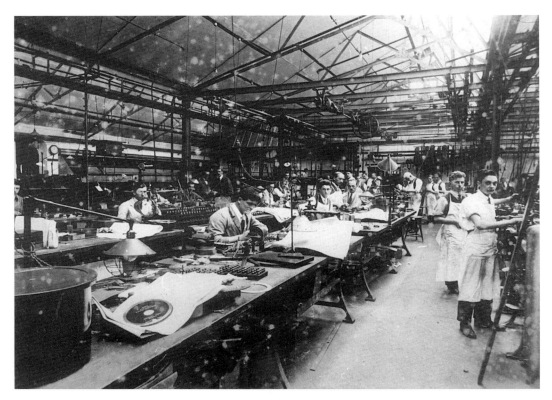

and Marshall sent his mechanics to try to repair it. Watching the giant flying machine was a fascinated eight-year-old boy, Marshall's son Arthur. On that day, a passion for planes was born in the young boy, a passion that was to find expression when he joined the family firm in the 1920s – and founded Cambridge Airport.

Two fellow entrepreneurs in Cambridge at the time were Donald Mackay, who established his hardware business in the town in 1912, and whose shop has remained in East Road ever since, and Cyril Ridgeon, who launched his builder's merchant company in 1911. At the time, most building supplies came into Cambridge by rail – and with great commercial acumen, Ridgeon decided to establish his business right next to the tracks.

Cambridge University's growing stature in science also helped to foster two firms which were not only to become big employers, but which were to make Cambridge's name famous around the world. One was the Cambridge Instrument Company, which became internationally known for making temperature-measuring instruments, seismographs, and medical equipment, such as electrocardiographs. The second was Pye's, founded by former Cavendish Lab worker W.G. Pye in the shed of his family home in Humberstone Road in 1896. By the start of World War One, it had grown into a large factory in Newmarket Road, making telescopes and height-finders for planes, and by the end of the war, it had begun to specialise in making a product that would soon be in almost every living room in the country, and which was to be one of the most enduring symbols of the 20th century – the wireless.

The growth of these businesses and the growth of the university were inextricably linked. As its scientific prowess swelled, the university needed specialised equipment to carry out its research, and the local firms expanded to meet that demand. Their own success then further enhanced Cambridge's name worldwide, and gave the university's science research added impetus. In the

Radio station – Pye's polishing shop.

previous century, new laboratories and museums had been opened in the town centre, and in 1904, the new King, Edward VII, came to open more facilities, the Botany Department, the Medical School and the Sidgwick Museum.

During these years, Cambridge was at the forefront of some of the century's most significant scientific discoveries. In 1901, J.N. Lanley demonstrated that adrenalin speeded up the heart. In 1906, Sir Frederick Gowland Hopkins, Professor of Biochemistry, made the first scientific study of vitamins, and went on to investigate enzymes, and how muscles work. Six years later, Lawrence Bragg, a physics student in his 20s, realised that X-rays could be diffracted, a breakthrough in the field of crystallography. The brainwave came to him while out for a walk on the Backs, and he went on to develop the discovery with his father Sir William Bragg, which won both men the Nobel Prize in 1915.

Following the opening of the Botany Department, two research organisations were founded in the city, which between them had a big impact on Britain's food-production industry. The Plant Breeding Institute and the National Institute of Agricultural Botany, established in 1911 and 1918 respectively, pioneered work on how to grow disease-free crops, research that was to be vital during the war years, and which has since been the cornerstone of modern dietetics.

In the first two decades of the 20th century, the number of undergraduates increased to nearly 4,000, and much of the town centre was occupied by university and college buildings. Among the students was Jawaharlal Nehru, who became Prime Minister of India in the 50s and 60s, and Ludwig Wittgenstein, who came to Cambridge from Vienna to study philosophy with Bertrand Russell. The two men, with G.E. Moore, made Cambridge the most important centre for the study of philosophy in the English-speaking world.

For many of the students, of course, being at university was as much about having a good time as getting down to serious study. Young, high-spirited, and with plenty of leisure time on their hands, undergraduates frequently took to the

streets for a bit of fun. Sometimes it was to ridicule those who had done less than brilliantly in their exams. The expression 'getting the wooden spoon', for example, refers to a real wooden spoon, traditionally awarded in a fake degree ceremony to the student who scored the lowest pass mark in the maths exam. Another popular pastime was the mock funeral, when hundreds of undergraduates, many dressed in silly costumes, organised a procession of vehicles and people through the town centre, aping a genuine funeral. The 'deceased' was usually a student sent down for a disciplinary offence. In one of the biggest such funerals, in 1911, a long parade of landaus, hansoms and taxis, led by a delivery van covered in crepe drapes, made its way through the town, the cap and gown of the `corpse' resting on the van's roof. The student himself, dressed in a grey suit and felt hat, sat in the middle, with a cartload of mourners behind. He was taken to the railway station, and the crowd of students gave him a riotous send-off, swarming all over the platform and climbing on the train.

On another occasion, in 1905, the Mayor of Cambridge got an important-looking telegram announcing that the Sultan of Zanzibar, in London on a visit, would arrive at the station in a few hours, and wanted to be escorted around the town and colleges. The Mayor sent a carriage to meet the visitors, and the royal party, in turbans and flowing white robes, duly arrived. Speaking an obscure language that no one understood, but which strangely had some words in common with English – such as the expletive

Getting the wooden spoon.

Distinguished visitors – a newspaper cartoon about the Zanzibar prank.

A mock funeral in 1911.

*Rag time in
Cambridge.*

uttered by one of them when he stubbed his toe – the royal party was given a tour of the colleges. Later, at the station, crowds gathered to see the royals depart – but instead of boarding the train, they leapt into a couple of hansom cabs and disappeared up Hills Road. It was, of course, all a gigantic hoax, perpetrated by students at Trinity.

One of the most violent forms of amusement was the Rag, where the students literally ran riot around the town, and got into pitched battles with police. In 1904, after the opening of new university buildings in Downing Street, undergraduates attempted to light a bonfire on Market Hill, and were charged by mounted constables. They were forced down Petty Cury, where a confectioner's window was smashed, and stock stolen. When they got to Parker's Piece, the young mob ripped down wooden railings from people's houses and started a bonfire. Police arrived in large numbers, and one young man was arrested. As he was dragged off to be locked up, the undergraduates besieged the police station. Local youths then became involved in the trouble, and another blaze was started in New Square, with trees and fences used as fuel. It took firemen until nearly midnight to dowse the flames. The following year, student riots erupted on Bonfire Night, and the university had to pay the town £200 to cover the cost of the damage caused.

The students' privileged lifestyles and high jinks were in sharp contrast to the plight of local youngsters from poorer families. Most schools were run privately, by boards and by churches, and many parents could not afford to pay the fees, even though they could be as little as twopence a week. Education covered the three Rs, reading, writing and arithmetic, but some boys' schools insisted youngsters did military-style drill as well.

In 1902, things changed for the better with the passing of the Education Act, which placed board schools under the control of local education authorities in boroughs and counties. For the first time, public money was used to pay for children's education, and the new authorities were given the power to set up secondary schools and technical schools, as well as develop elementary ones. In Cambridge, two county high schools were created, one in Hills Road for boys, in 1903, and the other for girls, originally in Collier Road, in 1908. It later moved to Long Road. The first newly-built council school, Romsey School, was opened in 1905. Four years later, Cambridge and County School of Arts, Crafts and Technology, the forerunner of today's Anglia Polytechnic University, opened too.

Improvements were also on the way in terms of people's health – and not before time. At the turn of the century, one in three families was reported to be living 'on the breadline', and diseases like smallpox were still rife, with children particularly at risk. In 1904, 107 youngsters aged under 12 months died in Cambridge – one in eight of the town's newborn babies. For those who survived, a lengthy recuperative stay on the children's ward at Addenbrooke's Hospital was often needed, and in the early years of the century, more than 1,300 patients a year were being treated there.

*Digging trenches for
the first electricity
cables.*

To meet the need, the hospital's facilities were increased. An operating theatre was installed, and by 1915, it had nearly 200 beds. Pathological laboratories, vital in combating disease, were also completed. The fight against child illnesses was fought in the community too. The Voluntary Association for Maternity and Child Welfare employed two health visitors to check on children's health at home, and in 1909, Cambridge became the first town in Britain to provide proper dental treatment for children of school age. A year later, a special depot supplying pasteurised milk was set up in Newmarket Road. Mothers could take their babies there to get milk, and have them weighed. Two years after that, four infant welfare centres were opened.

Laying the cables.

Something else that began to transform people's lives was electricity. The Cambridge Electric Supply Company, established in 1892, installed steam turbines at Thompson's Lane to generate the new power, and streets were dug up to accommodate underground cables. Colleges and businesses were the first to be connected, but soon public areas were too. Not many ordinary people took part in the big switch-on initially, however – with a light bulb costing the equivalent of £30 in today's money, it was a bit too pricey for many families.

Electric power boosted the newest form of entertainment, movies. Although films were still silent – the first talkie was not screened in Cambridge until 1929, *Broadway Melody*, starring Anita Page, Bessie Love and Charles King, at the Central – people flocked to see them. Theatres like the New Theatre, which put on variety performances, diversified into movies and were swamped with customers. Others that followed suit included The Empire, renamed the Kinema in 1916, and the Electric Theatre on Market Hill, later called the Victoria. The first purpose-built cinema in Cambridge was the Playhouse in Mill Road, which opened in 1912.

People still enjoyed more traditional entertainment as well. Fairs, such as Midsummer Fair, remained popular. Grazing cows were herded off Midsummer Common to make way for steam engines, and roundabouts with horses, camels

The Kinema, one of Cambridge's first cinemas.

and ostriches. On the edge of the common was the Circus of Varieties, with its jugglers and bizarre animal acts, including performing roosters. As well as the May boat races, punting became tremendously popular. 'Last year there was hardly a punt, and before that they were not known in Cambridge; yet this summer every boatyard possesses a flotilla,' the *Daily News* reported. People also loved swimming in the river. There was a segregated area for women to bathe, and men and boys used to take a dip at Sheep's Green and Coe Fen – in the nude. Passing women were urged to unfurl their parasols to avoid catching sight of the naked male bathers. The river could be a dangerous place, however. Ferries were used to get people from one side of the River Cam to the other, and in 1905, on the last day of the May races, an overcrowded vessel sank, claiming the lives of three women passengers. The tragedy renewed public demands for a bridge to be built at the Fort St George, and in 1913, the council agreed to do so, although it was another 14 years before it was finally erected.

Ferries were still needed in several places on the Cam.

In winter, there was skating. Cambridge and the Fens are said to be the birthplace of ice skating in England. For centuries, people in the area had fixed animal bones to their shoes to make skates, and proper metal-bladed skates came into use in the late 17th century. Village used to take on village, with money and food as prizes, and great champions came to the fore, such as 'Gutta Percha' See, George 'Fish' Jarman, and William 'Turkey' Smart, who died in 1919. The National Skating Association was founded by a Cambridge man, James Drake Digby, and it held championship meetings either at Swavesey,

Ice skating on frozen fields and rivers was a popular winter pursuit.

outside the town, or at Lingay Fen in Cambridge. Crowds of spectators came along to watch the contests, many travelling from a long way off, and there were international matches. As well as skating, the game of bandy was played regularly – an early form of ice hockey.

The town's commons were ideal for sports of all kinds. Butt Green, for example, got its name from the target butts that were placed on it for archery competitions. Cricket matches were played on Parker's Piece, and it was there that legendary players like England batsman Jack Hobbs cut their teeth. Hobbs notched up an incredible 197 centuries and 61,221 runs in first class cricket, and made his first century on Parker's Piece itself.

A cricket match on Parker's Piece, 1900.

The First Eastern General Hospital, at Trinity College.

On the wards at the war hospital.

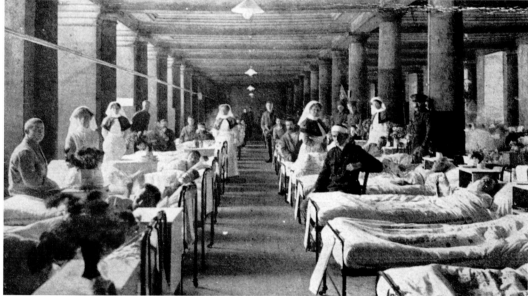

Between 1914 and 1918, more than 80,000 casualties were brought to Cambridge by train, and taken to the First Eastern General Hospital, established at Trinity College and in prefabricated buildings off West Road. At any one time, up to 800 soldiers were being looked after there. Many had horrific injuries inflicted by German machine guns on battlefields like the Somme. Others were suffering from the effects of inhaling poison gas, first unleashed by the Germans in 1915 on the Western Front.

One of the most famous victims of the war was Cambridge poet Rupert Brooke. Educated at King's College, he became the most popular romantic symbol of the pre-war years, admired not only for the beauty of his writing, but for his good looks.

One of his most celebrated poems, about his time in Cambridge, was *The Old Vicarage, Grantchester*, which contained the famous lines: 'Stands the Church clock at ten to three? And is there honey still for tea'. During World War One, Brooke became a commissioned officer in the Royal Naval Division, and saw the toll in human life that was being exacted. He wrote, in his poem *The Soldier*: 'If I should die, think only this of me: That there's some corner of a foreign field That is for ever England.' In 1915, en route to a posting in the Dardanelles, he suffered blood poisoning from a mosquito bite, and died, aged just 28.

Tragic poet – Rupert Brooke.

When Germany finally surrendered, and the Armistice was signed on November 11, 1918, people took to the streets of Cambridge to celebrate. Shops and workplaces closed, and pubs were packed with revellers. A month or so later, Britain celebrated the first Christmas for four years without war – and Cambridge played a big part in reflecting the nation's joy that the conflict was over. For the first time, the Festival of Nine Lessons and Carols, the famous service from King's College Chapel on Christmas Eve, was broadcast.

Peace celebrations after World War One.

Trams and bicycles were the main method of getting around in Cambridge after the war. There were several retailers of bicycles, such as Howes and Herbert Robinson, and cycling clubs were formed, staging regular events in and around the town. Before the turn of the century, there were so many cyclists on the roads, many of them going too fast, according to the authorities, that it had even been suggested that cyclists should have their own roads – cycle lanes. However, as the 1920s dawned, new forms of transport were starting to take over the streets.

Motor buses had been introduced as early as 1905, when two rival bus companies came into being, travelling the same route and competing for the same passengers.

*Home at last –
demobbed soldiers
march through the
town, 1919.*

*Pedal power –
warning to cyclists to
slow down.*

On the first day, 2,000 brave souls climbed aboard the buses – one painted in Cambridge's colour, light blue, and the other in Oxford's, dark blue – to travel from the railway station into the town centre. One of the buses was an open top double decker, and from it passengers could see things previously hidden, which later prompted protests from undergraduates with first-floor rooms. Pedestrians were also worried about the black smoke the buses belched out, the noise of their engines, and the speed they travelled – a cartoon at the time showed a bus running over a dog, hitting a lamppost, and scaring ladies on their bikes. Within six months, the double decker had been banned, and soon afterward, the other bus was forced off the road too. Two years later, however, a new company came on the scene, Ortona, and bus travel really did take off. By the 1920s, bus routes criss-crossed most of the town and there were routes outside it too, supporting Cambridge's aspirations to be a regional shopping centre. At first, the bus terminus was outside the Senate House, but then a new bus station was built in Drummer Street.

Borough of Cambridge.

NOTICE TO CYCLISTS

COMPLAINTS having been made of the dangerous rate of speed at which CYCLISTS proceed through the Streets of the Borough, especially those portions of the Streets which are paved with asphalte, and of their neglecting to sound a bell or whistle or otherwise giving audible and sufficient warning of their approach,

Notice is Hereby Given,

that the Police Authorities have been specially instructed to take proceedings against all persons riding

Bicycles and Tricycles

at such a rate of speed as to endanger the life or limb of any passenger, or failing to give sufficient warning of their approach in the manner above indicated.

By Order of the Watch Committee,

J. E. L. WHITEHEAD,

Town Clerk.

GUILDHALL, CAMBRIDGE,
May, 1895.

Within a few more years, cars and motorcycles were also everywhere. The first car in Cambridge had cruised serenely into the

changed society's view of how economies should be managed, and of the literary critic F.R. Leavis, who wrote *New Bearings in English Poetry*, and whose thoughts on the English language influenced generations of students.

While the university's geniuses were pushing back the boundaries of science, Cambridge engineering company Pye, already making 40,000 wireless sets a year, branched out into a second, even more exciting new medium – television. Demonstrations of John Logie Baird's invention took place at the Royal Institution in 1926, and the BBC – established in 1927 – transmitted test signals three years later. The early sets only had tiny screens – one measured just four inches square – and picture quality was pretty poor. Nevertheless, people were fascinated. In 1937, big queues built up when the coronation of George VI was shown in Cambridge – on a TV set in a tent in Sedley Taylor Road. Pye was the principal manufacturer of the set's vital component the cathode ray tube, and the company began turning out thousands of sets. By the early 1950s, it was Britain's biggest manufacturer.

Television was a symbol of modernity and affluence, but there were millions of people for whom owning such a luxury was an impossible dream. The Depression of the 1920s and 1930s plunged many families into crisis. Men lost their jobs, and most people had to tighten their belts. Shopping was restricted to essentials – and the suicide rate went up. In a bid to ease the situation, the Government appealed to people to sell gold, jewellery and other items to raise money – and then spend the cash, in the theory that it would get the economy moving. 'This is the time to spend – buy new clothes, furniture, or extra food,' the *Daily News* reported at the time. 'Have your house decorated or painted. A prompt response will lift thousands of homes from misery into happiness by Christmas.'

Moves to cut miners' wages and make them work longer triggered the General Strike in 1926. Miners' leader A.J. Cook declared 'Not a penny off the pay, not a minute on the day', and the Trades Union Congress called out transport workers, printers, builders, industrial workers and engineers. The stoppage cut no ice with

Railwaymen on strike in Cambridge, 1926.

Montage from the Daily News, showing students running trains during the General Strike.

Strike Scenes : Cambridg

[Chronicle Photos.]

the middle classes – or students in Cambridge. In the 'Red Romsey' area across Mill Road bridge, railwaymen had stopped work, but in true-blue central Cambridge, the university gave undergraduates time off from their studies so they could rally to the call for volunteers to keep the country going. More than 2,000 students did so. Upper-class young gentlemen were soon seen working as labourers, keeping the peace as special constables, and – fulfilling many a schoolboy dream – driving trains. Daily carloads of strikebreakers set off from the Backs to strike-bound areas all over the country. Most students found the work hard, but good fun. It was also better than the alternative drudgery of swotting for exams. They did not always do a good job. On one occasion, a train driven by students came off the rails near Mill

Road bridge, and hundreds of strikers turned out to mock the inexperienced young drivers.

In 1932, there were more than 1,600 men out of work in Cambridge alone. A third of these were men from the building trade – and it was this that eventually helped the town get back on the road to prosperity. In the immediate years after the war, many people were living in slum conditions, without sanitation – even in relatively well-heeled Cambridge. In some areas, such as Gothic Street and Doric Street, the *Daily News* reported that people's health was being affected, especially children's. The first borough council homes in Cambridge, 100 of them, were built in 1920 in Cavendish Avenue, Hills Avenue, and Hinton Avenue. Then in 1927, Cambridge Housing Society put up its first family homes, in Green End Road. In the 1930s, hundreds of the town's jobless men were put to work on further construction schemes and slum clearance, paid for with Government subsidies provided under the 1930 Housing Act.

New homes in Green End Road, 1927.

The 1930s saw new accommodation for the two principal local authorities in Cambridgeshire, Cambridge's own borough council, and the county council. In 1931, a new Shire Hall was built for the county council, using the site of the former County Gaol on Castle Hill, and materials from it too. Before the gaol was demolished, an open day was held, so that people could have a look around it – and 8,000 visitors turned up. Two years later, the go-ahead was given for a new Guildhall in the market square for the Cambridge authority. The old Guildhall dated back to 1782, and in 1897, a spectacular design for a new one had been put forward, but turned down. It was not until 1933 that a rebuilding scheme got the go-ahead, and work started on it in 1935, with completion in 1939. Cambridge needed bigger and better municipal buildings because it was continuing to grow. In 1934, the borough boundaries had been extended to take in Cherry Hinton and Trumpington. Not everyone was in favour of expanding the town, of course. In 1928, Cambridge Preservation Society was founded, amid concerns that development was out of control.

Shire Hall, new headquarters of Cambridgeshire County Council.

The new Guildhall, completed in 1939.

The economic ups-and-downs made people yearn for a little escapism and entertainment, and this led to a flurry of new cinemas and theatres in Cambridge. Thanks to the public's passion for silent movie stars like Charlie Chaplin and Rudolph Valentino, Cambridge saw the Tivoli open in 1925, and the Victoria in 1931. The curtain came up on the Festival Theatre in 1926, and 10 years later, Cambridge Arts Theatre opened.

The innovative Festival Theatre in Newmarket Road was founded by Terence Gray, who wanted

Curtain up – the Festival Theatre, pictured in 1929.

Cambridge Arts Theatre.

to try out new ideas about sets, stage lighting and other production techniques, and many pioneering performances were staged there. The Arts Theatre's mentor was John Maynard Keynes. He was a Fellow and later bursar of King's College, and he used his own money to get the theatre off the ground. Not only did he pay for the site, he even sat in the box office selling tickets in the early years.

Sport also cheered up the town during the 1920s and 1930s. In the Paris Olympics of 1924, two Cambridge runners were in the British team, Arthur Marshall, son of the founder of the city's engineering company, and Harold Abrahams, a law student at the university. The two runners were pals, but it was Abrahams who was to win glory. He reached the 100m final, and in an amazing run, beat the world record holder Charley Paddock to win gold for Britain. Another British runner, Eric Liddell, bemused officials by backing out of the 100 metres because of religious convictions – the heats were held on a Sunday. However, he triumphed in the 400m instead, setting a new record. The exploits of Liddell and Abrahams were immortalised in the movie *Chariots of Fire*, part of which was filmed in Cambridge, and today the city hosts an annual charity relay run with the same title.

Arthur Marshall watching the Chariots of Fire relay run.

Opening of Jesus Green outdoor pool in 1923 – the opening ceremony featured a series of races.

In 1932, Abbey Football Club, Cambridge United's forerunner, opened a new ground in Newmarket Road. Other places of entertainment that appeared in the town were Jesus Green public swimming pool in 1923, and the Dorothy, which became the in place for eating out – and dancing. The three-storey building spanning the space between Sidney Street and Hobson Street opened in 1931. The ground floor entrance led to a shop, showroom, and a restaurant. On the first floor was a dance hall with a black hornbeam floor on springs, which could accommodate 450 dancers. On the floor above was a dining hall for private clubs and other organisations. There was also a roof garden overlooking the gardens of Christ's College and in the basement, a pub, the Prince of Wales. The complex was the brainchild of George Hawkins, who also owned a bakery and several bread shops, and when it opened, thousands flocked there.

Cambridge University library under construction in 1934.

The newly-established airport was not a key defensive installation. It only had a couple of machine guns for its own protection, one on its control tower, and the other a mobile one. Luckily, however, it was only attacked on a couple of occasions. The airport's principal role was in training pilots, and repairing military planes. At one stage, more than 180 training aircraft, mainly Tiger Moths, were based there, and during the war, about 20,000 pilots, instructors and observers were trained – a vital element in the Allies' eventual victory. The airport carried out repair and

Bomber repair team at Marshall's during the war.

rebuilding work on more than 5,000 planes, including Hurricanes, Blenheims, and the famed Spitfires.

While Marshall's did its bit for the war effort, Pye was also bringing its engineering skills to bear. The Cambridge company worked flat out to produce radio and radar equipment for the armed forces.

In 1941, the Germans invaded Russia, and then the Japanese bombed Pearl Harbor, bringing America into the war. A few months later, the first United States Air Force fliers began to arrive in Britain, to join the aerial assault on Hitler's forces in Europe.

Many joined RAF crews at airfields in Cambridgeshire, including Duxford and Wyton. Soon, American airmen were a common sight in Cambridge. Dubbed 'over-paid, over-sexed, and over here', they were much better-off than their British hosts, and were free with their money, spending much of it in the local pubs, paying for local children's parties at Christmas, and furnishing local girls with something they desperately desired – nylons. One of their most popular haunts in Cambridge was a place they called Bull College – the Bull Hotel, which had become an American Red Cross service club. Cambridge's sacred cricket ground, Fenner's, was even used as the venue for a baseball match between two US army teams, the Kentucky Rebels and the Yankee Eagles. Romances blossomed between the 'Yanks' and Cambridge girls, and after the war, many American servicemen went back to the States with Fenland brides.

Women worked in the fields to keep the farming industry going while the men were away fighting. In Cambridgeshire, the Women's Land Army was augmented with girls from the industrial north, Manchester and Leeds. They were up at the crack of dawn, planting and tending crops of vegetables and cereals. It was part of the Government's Dig For Victory campaign, aimed at boosting food production.

Although Cambridge had acquired plenty of new shops in the 1920s and 1930s – Sainsbury's in 1925, and Marks & Spencer in 1934 – the war left them with

Americans in Cambridge, 1944 – United States military men were a common sight in the town.

Bull College – the Bull Hotel, which the US airmen made their base.

Fighting fit – Land Army girls at Burwell, near Cambridge.

The American Cemetery at Madingley, opened in 1944.

precious little to sell. Rationing had been introduced, and people had to use coupons to buy food, clothes and other items. There were shortages right through the war, which continued in the years immediately after it too. At a moment's notice, people had to be ready to run for the safety of the public air-raid shelters, under Peas Hill, and in the strongrooms of Lloyds Bank. Ready-made shelters could be bought, for £7 10s. Sandbags were piled up against buildings, and windows were taped to prevent them being shattered by the impact of bombs. There was a blackout every night, and kerbs were painted white so people could spot them more easily in the dark. Any resident who showed a light after dark was liable to a fine of up to £500 – or two years' imprisonment. Home Guard forces were mobilised, both in the town and in the villages around it, armed with 2,000 .303 rifles which arrived in Cambridge in May 1940.

Most families had a loved one away from home, in the Army, Royal Navy or RAF. It was a time of terrible privation, as well as worry, for those left behind. Many had evacuees living with them, meals had to be conjured from next to nothing, and there was the constant fear that those fighting in the war might not come back. The wives and daughters of men serving in the Cambridgeshire Regiment suffered more than most. The soldiers were captured in 1942 at the fall of Singapore, and their captors, the Japanese, treated them with great brutality. Many died in jails like Changi, or on forced marches through the jungle. It was little wonder that after the war, those who survived were given the Freedom of the Borough on their return to Cambridge.

The town played host to senior Allied commanders in the Spring of 1944. General Dwight Eisenhower and Field Marshal Bernard Montgomery met secretly at a Cambridge college to discuss the operation that was to lead to the end of the war – the D-Day landings in Normandy by British, American and Canadian troops. A model of the beaches was constructed for them to study. In the event, the assault did not take place on the day decided, but was postponed until June. On the day it should have happened, however, a lasting tribute was inaugurated to the Americans who had lost their lives flying bombing missions from the area – the American Cemetery at Madingley was opened.

Fighter planes from Duxford were among those providing air cover for the invasion fleet, and after fighting their way through France, the Allies liberated Paris, and in 1945, crossed the Rhine. A month later, they reached Berlin – and on 7 May Germany finally surrendered. In Cambridge, as in other towns and cities, work stopped, licensing laws were suspended, and people took to the streets,

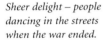

Sheer delight – people dancing in the streets when the war ended.

VE-Day celebrations – the official party on the balcony of the Guildhall.

dancing, kissing and hugging each other. In towns and cities, there were street parties and fireworks as Britain celebrated VE-Day – Victory in Europe.

The *Cambridge Daily News* reported: 'All over the world, VE-Day has evoked expressions of thankfulness and joy. Mr Churchill, in his end-of-the-war broadcast this afternoon, stated that hostilities will cease one minute after midnight.'

In the immediate years after the war, Cambridge saw a number of improvements in transport, schools, and hospital services. The town had a long history of traffic problems. Even in the days when hansom cabs plied the streets, there were numerous accidents, some caused by crazy driving, and some by the antics of students. At the start of term, for example, the cabmen – many of whom used ex-racing horses from nearby Newmarket – would pick up students at the station to take them to their colleges, and would open their apron doors at the back so their passengers could drag their bicycles along behind. By 1930, many undergraduates had their own cars, but the growing number of vehicles clogging the streets led to a ban on students owning them. After the war, Cambridge pioneered a new solution to road congestion. It was the first town in the country to start using something we now take for granted – radio-controlled taxis.

Education in Cambridge – and the nation as a whole – took a step forward thanks to R.A. Butler, MP for nearby Saffron Walden. Butler was the son of Sir Montague Butler, Master of Pembroke College, and was Minister of Education between 1941 and 1945. It was he who steered through the 1944 Education Act, which established three types of free secondary education – in grammar schools, secondary modern schools, and technical schools. With an '11 plus' exam, it set the pattern for state education in England and Wales for the next two decades. In Cambridge, secondary modern schools included Chesterton and Coleridge, and St George's Church of England school in Barnwell. Parkside

R.A. Butler.

was one of the technical schools. Butler went on to hold a succession of top Cabinet posts, including Chancellor of the Exchequer, Home Secretary, Foreign Secretary, and Deputy Prime Minister. He later became Master of Trinity College.

Coleridge school.

Parkside, one of the new technical schools in the 1940s.

Soon after the new schools system was introduced, the National Health Service came into being as well. It was established in 1946 under an Act of Parliament, but did not actually get under way until 1948. Health Minister Aneurin Bevan declared that its aim was to provide a comprehensive system of health care for everyone, free at the point of delivery. Free prescriptions were introduced, and local councils began to provide midwifery services, home nursing for those who needed it, and vaccinations.

At the same time, the Government brought in National Insurance and other welfare schemes to help jobless people and the elderly.

In Cambridge, the NHS was a godsend for poorer people. Before the service was created, people even had to pay a fare to be taken to hospital by ambulance – 1s 3d a mile, or 6p in today's money. In 1947, Cambridgeshire ambulance service became the first to carry patients free of charge, and by 1949, a Government report stated that 'Cambridge is among the healthiest of the larger towns of England.'

The year 1947 was also memorable for having one of the worst winters anyone could remember. There were heavy snowstorms and freezing temperatures for weeks, and in some areas, snowdrifts were 20ft high. Food had to be dropped to villages by air, fuel shortages soon developed, and thousands of workers were laid off because of power cuts. After the big freeze came widespread flooding. On 14 March, the *Daily News* reported that Cambridge had been seriously hit: 'The rapidly rising and flowing river has invaded riverside homes, Midsummer Common and other open spaces are flooded, there have been fears for the safety of Silver Street bridge, and there is no sign of any diminution of the abnormal flow.'

The icy atmosphere between male-dominated Cambridge University and the women campaigning for equal academic rights also thawed out that same year. Two colleges for women, Girton and Newnham, had opened in the third quarter of the 19th century, but attempts to make women full members of the university had been continually thwarted by the male-dominated establishment. In 1897, crowds of male undergraduates had gathered outside the Senate House to lobby a vote on the issue, and were delighted when it was rejected. They dangled a female

Homes in Cambridge were inundated during the disastrous 1947 floods.

The Queen Mother, then the Queen, in Cambridge in 1948 to receive her honorary degree.

dummy on a bicycle from a nearby bookshop window. Then in 1921, there were more turbulent scenes outside the Senate House when admitting women was debated again, and turned down. A huge banner outside read: 'Here's no place for you maids'. However, in 1947, the cause of equality at last prevailed. Both Girton and Newnham Colleges were admitted to the university – and women students got full equal status with men. The first female graduations were put off, however, until the year after. The university wanted the first woman to get a degree to be the Queen, now the Queen Mother. In October 1948, she duly became the first woman to do so, receiving a Doctor of Laws degree.

Alongside this social revolution, further remarkable changes were brewing in the university's research labs, and in the labs of engineering company Pye.

The firm came up with a system of relaying pictures from cameras at fixed points, and demonstrated it by beaming pictures of Cambridge traffic to a road safety exhibition held at the Corn Exchange. It was a world first.

At the university, groundbreaking work was carried out in the development of computers. In 1946, an electronic brain was created by a team of experts in America, one of whom was Prof Douglas Hartree of Cambridge. Called ENIAC, the Electronic Numerical Integrator and Computer, it was huge – 18ft high, 80 ft long, and weighing 30 tons. By modern standards, it was slower than a modest laptop, but it worked a thousand times faster than the previous calculating machine, the Harvard Mark 1. One of its early roles was to do the calculations necessary for the creation of the hydrogen bomb.

Then came EDSAC, the Electronic Delay Storage Automatic Calculator, developed by a team led by Cambridge scientist Maurice Wilkes, who was in charge of the university's computer laboratory. This was the first stored program digital computer to work successfully, and it could achieve a calculating speed 15,000 times faster than the human brain – a milestone in the development of today's computers.

Prof Maurice Wilkes, right, computer pioneer, pictured looking at a memory board in the 1970s.

City Status

I T HAD taken a long time coming but finally, at the start of the 1950s, Cambridge officially became a city. Seven and a half centuries before, in 1201, King John had granted Cambridge its first charter, setting it on the road to expansion and greater independence from the Crown. The town had grown from a settlement of just three or four thousand people to one of nearly 90,000. Most people regarded it, as opposed to Norwich or Ipswich, as the capital of East Anglia – and it was of course home to one of the world's biggest universities.

In 1951, Cambridge's councillors sent a petition to the then-King, George VI, spelling out how important Cambridge was in the region, how big it had become, what it had achieved culturally, academically, and economically – and asking for it to be given city status. Most people were not very hopeful of success. A similar request had been made in the past – admittedly some time before, in 1617 – and that had been turned down flat. However, George VI did grant the petition, and only a week after receiving it. In the early hours of Saturday 24 March 1951, a statement was released in London, which said: 'The King… has been graciously pleased to confer on the Borough of Cambridge the title and dignity of a city.' In celebration, the Union Jack was hoisted above the Guildhall, and the bells of Great St Mary's church rang out during the day.

In April, less than a month after making Cambridge a city, the King came for a visit. He had been a student in Cambridge for a year, between 1919 and 1920, and he had unveiled the town's war memorial, so he knew the city well. His visit in 1951 was intended to mark the replacement of King's College Chapel's stained glass windows, removed for fear of damage during the war, but crowds turned out to cheer their gratitude for the fact that Cambridge's importance in the 20th century had at last been recognised.

Two years later, George VI was dead, and his daughter, Elizabeth, was crowned Queen. In 1955, she too visited Cambridge, and smiled and waved to a huge crowd from the balcony of the Guildhall.

The year of the Queen's coronation was an exciting one for science, thanks to the

The young Queen, on the balcony of the Guildhall, 1955.

brilliance of two Cambridge researchers, Francis Crick and James Watson. Crick, a biologist, and Watson, an American zoologist, had been trying to find out more about deoxyribonucleic acid – DNA – the basic genetic material of all living organisms. They wanted to know how genes replicated, and passed on hereditary characteristics from parent to offspring. In 1953, working in a Cambridge lab, the two men succeeded in describing the structure of the molecule that transmits those characteristics, a structure which they called the Double Helix. Without a doubt, it was one of the great scientific breakthroughs of all time. Their work helped lay the foundations for molecular biology, and all kinds of later research into inherited diseases.

Crick and Watson were not the only Cambridge men to change the course of science that year. Fred Sanger, a chemist working at Cambridge's Medical Research Council laboratories, successfully completed the first full chemical analysis of a protein, insulin, a major step in understanding the structure of proteins and nucleic acids. In another MRC lab, molecular biologist Max Perutz and his student

Secret of life – Crick and Watson in 1953.

John Kendrew, carried out ground-breaking work on haemoglobin, the red oxygen-carrying pigment in the blood. All five men were later to be awarded Nobel Prizes.

1953 is also remembered in Cambridge as the year of one of the worst weather disasters ever – the East Coast floods. On the night of January 31, a vast tidal surge swept across the North Sea, bursting through the East Coast's sea defences. Whipped up by gale-force winds, the wall of water gushed inland, destroying hundreds of buildings in its path. Within a few hours, 150,000 acres of farmland had been swamped, 40,000 people had been driven out of their homes – and 300 had drowned. People clung to the roofs of their houses as water swirled below, and many took to boats. The floodwaters did little damage in Cambridge itself, but the city became a major centre for the rescue operations. The Women's Voluntary Service in Cambridge mobilised hundreds of helpers, taking over a former aircraft hangar at Madingley on the outskirts of the city to pack up donated clothing for the flood victims, and undergraduates from Cambridge University joined policemen, servicemen and river workers to close a breach in the banks of the Ouse, near King's Lynn.

The 1950s and 1960s were heady times for Cambridge. After the austerity of the war years, people suddenly found they had more money in their pockets. In the 1950s, rationing ended, wages rose, central heating came in, and new homes were built. The first house on Cambridge's Arbury council estate went up in 1955. Sales of household goods like TVs and washing machines shot up – the *Daily News* reported in 1952 that one in five of the city's houses had TV aerials, and city firm Pye was Britain's biggest manufacturer of TV sets. Home furnishings were big sellers, and there was a boom in leisure activities like swimming: Cambridge's Parkside Pool

Pye was Britain's biggest manufacturer of TV sets.

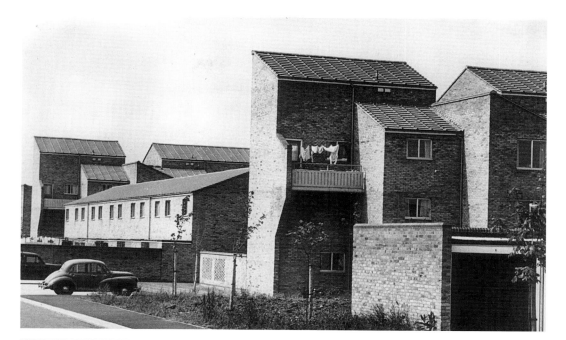

opened in 1963. Foreign holidays took off, and locally, whole streets set off on coach trips to the seaside.

Greater prosperity, however, also meant greater pressure for development, and it was at this time that a debate took place about the future of the city. Some businesses and councillors believed Cambridge had to carry on growing, but others, the majority, felt too much growth would be damaging, especially to the university. In 1950, a report was produced for the county council by the architectural practice Sir William Holford and Partners, which supported the latter view. It proposed limiting the expansion of the city and its closest villages, and instead encouraging growth in villages further away, the so-called 'necklace villages'. This plan was later endorsed by the Government, and a ring of sacrosanct land was established around the city, the Green Belt, where housing and business development was forbidden.

The first residents at Bar Hill.

In the 1960s, a new village was created to serve Cambridge's growing population – Bar Hill. It was the first purpose-built village to be established in England for more than a century, and was built in four phases. 'Careful planning will ensure that the tradition of Cambridgeshire villages is maintained – the close grouping of houses, a contrast between the village and the open countryside, with compact grouping encouraging pedestrian movement rather than vehicular,' the newspaper reported in 1963. The first houses built, in Acorn Avenue, cost just over £4,700, and they sold fast. Today Bar Hill has more than 5,000 residents.

If Cambridge's elders were trying to halt the march of progress and keep the world at bay, the same could not be said of the city's young people. They wanted change, and a new, more exciting lifestyle. The first of the post-war youth movements, the Teddy Boys, with their drainpipe trousers and velvet-collared jackets, was very much in evidence in Cambridge in the 1950s. Older people disliked them intensely, as much for their behaviour as their uninhibited style of dress. In local dance halls, where they jived to the rock 'n' roll of Bill Haley, trouble often erupted. Cambridge magistrates banned the movie featuring Haley's music in the mid-1950s, after cinema seats were ripped up by Teddy Boys.

The big pop stars of the time, such as Cliff Richard and Adam Faith, attracted massive crowds when they performed in the city, and police had trouble controlling the hysterical teenage girls who tried to mob their idols. The same thing happened when The Beatles played a concert in Cambridge in 1963. The Fab Four's album Please Please Me was at the top of the album charts, and they had to have a police escort when they arrived at the Regal Cinema. More than 4,000 fans, mainly screaming girls, besieged the venue, and after the show, The Beatles had to be smuggled out using a decoy police van. The newspaper, then renamed the

Drainpipes and velvet – Teddy Boys in Cambridge.

Cambridge News, reported: 'It took the four young Beatles less than a minute to run down a flight of stairs back-stage and scramble into their van. As soon as police sergeant Arthur Quinney, who was driving the van, pulled away from the

Adam Faith concert, 1960.

kerbside, the decoy Black Maria, with headlamps blazing, headed towards the crowds of teenagers.'

Cambridge's students were not so quick to latch on to the new music, or the new fashions. They were not averse to a bit of humorous misbehaviour, of course. In 1958, for example, the city woke up to discover an Austin 7 van sitting on the roof of the Senate House. It had been dismantled by students, carried up there in pieces, and completely rebuilt during the night, a prank to celebrate May Week. In general, however, the university's upper-crust image and strong links with the Establishment meant change was not welcome in many colleges, and most students toed the line. One or two switched to casual wear, such as jeans and duffel coats, but most carried on dressing in smart suits and ties, in the traditional dark, staid colours. Most, of course, were destined for jobs in the City, or with law firms, the Civil Service, and the Diplomatic Service.

Not all of them, however, subscribed to the accepted political structure of the time. Communism, for example, had great intellectual appeal to many, because it seemed to offer a fairer, more egalitarian society, and there was no doubt that some felt a little guilty about the privileged lives they led at university. It was these views that led to the so-called Cambridge spy scandal of the 1950s. Since the 1930s, the Russians had been trying to recruit agents among the university's bright young men, and by 1951, a number of former students were working for the Diplomatic Service – and actively spying for Moscow. Two of them were Donald MacLean and

Guy Burgess, who had been attached to the service's Washington office. MI5 suspected the pair were spies, and was about to expose them, but they were tipped off, and they defected to Russia. The man who alerted them to the threat of exposure was another Cambridge graduate, Kim Philby, who was working for British intelligence, but who was also an agent for the Russians. After Burgess and MacLean vanished, Philby was recalled to London for questioning, and later resigned from MI6, but he continued to pass on secrets to Russia until 1963, when he too defected to Moscow. The undercover

Cambridge spy Guy Burgess.

trio were supported by a fourth Cambridge spy ring member, Anthony Blunt. Blunt had been recruited as an agent at Cambridge by Burgess, and he too had gone on to join the British Secret Service. A brilliant art historian, he had been appointed as Surveyor of the Queen's Pictures, and although the authorities suspected him of espionage, he did not confess to it until 1964. In exchange for immunity from prosecution, he gave information to British intelligence, and was not officially unmasked until 1979, when Prime Minister Margaret Thatcher confirmed to MPs that he had been a spy.

Bust of Churchill at Churchill College.

The clampdown on commercial and housing development in the city signalled by the Holford report did not stop Cambridge University growing. Between the end of the war and the start of the 1960s, the number of people going to university doubled – and Cambridge had to expand to meet demand. A string of new colleges was added to the academic roll – New Hall in 1954, and in the 1960s, Churchill (named after the man who had led Britain during the war, Winston Churchill), St Edmund's, Darwin, Wolfson (at first called University College), Lucy Cavendish, Clare Hall, and Fitzwilliam.

There were other new buildings, too, including one that was to be the most controversial modern building in Cambridge – the History Faculty, completed in 1968.

Built on the Sidgwick site, it was designed by Sir James Stirling, and its glass and red brick structure was heavily criticised, one expert branding it 'actively ugly'. Despite the brickbats, the building won an architectural award in 1970, but went on to be plagued by faults. It was too hot in summer, too cold in winter, the roof leaked – and tiles kept falling off the walls. The university considered demolishing it completely in later years, but opted instead for extensive repairs.

The History Faculty's most famous student of the 1960s was Prince Charles, who came up to Trinity College in 1967. Unlike previous royals who had attended the university, he was determined to work for a degree. At first he was very much in the media spotlight, although this later diminished, and he was able to get on with his studies relatively unhindered. He was often seen walking through the streets to lectures, a freedom that would be unthinkable in today's security-conscious world.

New Hall, opened in 1954.

Churchill College dining hall.

Wolfson College.

Fitzwilliam College.

The Prince participated fully in college life, taking part in student Rag stunts, and even going on stage at the ADC Theatre for a comedy revue in which he was famously photographed in a dustbin.

The 1960s saw formal links develop between Cambridge and its German counterpart Heidelberg, like Cambridge famous for its university and its printing industry. The Heidelberg Link, an agreement of friendship, was drawn up in 1965. About this time, Cambridge University Press opened a big new print works in Shaftesbury Road, and the Cambridge News moved to new premises in Newmarket Road, changing its name to the *Cambridge Evening News* in 1969. That same year, Cambridge homes got North Sea gas, a little earlier than most other parts of the UK. The city was given priority for the conversion – because a number of depressed students had used the older, less safe gas to commit suicide.

Theatre and music thrived in Cambridge in the 1960s and 1970s. As well as the ADC, which had begun in 1855 as the university's Amateur Dramatic Club, Cambridge Arts Theatre established a reputation for nurturing talented actors who later went on to fame and fortune. After the death of Keynes in 1946, another

Controversial – the History Faculty.

King's College man had taken up the reins as the theatre's chairman, George 'Dadie' Rylands, and he helped steer the early careers of actors like Michael Redgrave, Jonathan Miller, Daniel Massey, and Derek Jacobi. Cambridge University's annual *Footlights* revue also produced many big-name stars. *The Goodies'* Bill Oddie and Tim Brooke-Taylor, John Cleese, and the likes of David Frost and Clive James all numbered among its performers in their 20s. One Footlights programme described Oddie as 'constitutionally unsociable and unenthusiastic. His only interest is ornithology.' Another star was Peter Cook, who appeared in the revue in 1959, and the same year, an undergraduate who was to go on to become Britain's most erudite quizmaster – Bamber Gascoigne, former host of TV's *University Challenge*. Cleese went on to team up with a group of Oxford graduates to launch the anarchic, cult TV comedy *Monty Python's Flying Circus*.

On the music scene, two big festivals brought thousands of people streaming into Cambridge. The Cambridge Festival began in 1961

Coronation – Prince Charles crowning the Rag Queen in 1969.

Prince Charles getting his degree in 1970.

Rubbish performance – the Prince on stage at the ADC.

Folk dancers from Heidelberg on the lawns of King's College, 1963.

with a handful of concerts and a historical pageant, but soon grew into a fortnight-long spectacular which included drama and visual arts as well as music. Among the performers were Sir Adrian Boult and the London Philharmonic, as well as many of Europe's most famous orchestras.

A hugely popular classical event was the madrigals on the river, held during the summer. Thousands of people, many on punts, turned out to hear the music. The other big festival was Cambridge Folk Festival, launched at Cherry Hinton Hall in

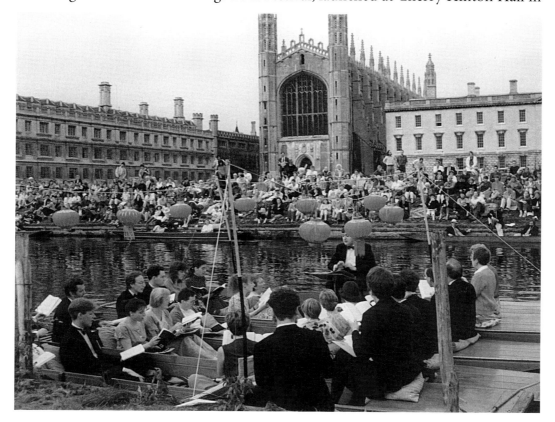

Water music – Cambridge Festival performance on the River Cam.

Cambridge Folk Festival.

Strawberry Fair.

1965. For three days in August, fans camped out to hear acts like Fairport Convention, The Dubliners, Tom Paxton, Al Stewart, Steeleye Span, and Ralph McTell, and the festival became one of the premier events in Europe and America.

In 1969, a free pop festival was held on Midsummer Common, which turned out to be the forerunner of what is now one of Cambridge's biggest summer events – Strawberry Fair. The fair itself did not start until 1974, when it featured jazz and folk concerts, with the profits going to local children's charities. It soon became one of the most popular events in the city calendar, with the music being complemented by hundreds of stalls selling everything from food to homemade crafts. Many of the stallholders – and those who came to hear the music – were what one writer described as 'people of the alternative society', the hippies of the 1960s and 1970s, who came from far and wide with Bedouin-style tents and brightly-painted vans and buses. The kind of music they loved was that produced by rock bands like Pink Floyd, in which two Cambridge-born men were key figures. Syd Barrett dreamed up the band's name, originally the Pink Floyd Sound, after American blues musicians Pink Anderson and Floyd Council, and was its main creative force in the late 1960s – participating in the classic albums *The Piper At The Gates of Dawn*, *A Saucerful of Secrets*, and *Ummagumma*, which included the song Grantchester Meadows. Barrett left the group in 1968, but in that year another Cambridge man joined up, Dave Gilmour.

Miss South Africa speaking in a Union Society debate.

Post-exam exuberance – the May Balls were a time to relax and clown about.

The morning after – sleeping off the night's excesses.

in June, where they dressed up, drank, and danced the night away, before sleeping it off for most of the following day. The exams, naturally, were tough, and until the 1970s, so was discipline by the colleges. Undergraduates were subject to gate hours and guest hours – set hours by which they had to be back at college in the evening, and by which guests in their rooms must depart. Policing them were a team of archaic university officials, the Proctor and his men, known as 'bulldogs'. The Students' Union fought a fierce campaign in the early 1970s to get these restrictions abolished.

Proctor and bulldogs on the march.

Students were not the only people in Cambridge to be protesting. Hundreds of townsfolk got on their bikes and staged a two-wheeled demonstration in the city in 1971, to highlight their disgust at the increase in car traffic.

Cycle protest – hundreds turn to pedal power.

The middle of Cambridge was transformed by a big new shopping development in the 1970s – Lion Yard. In the 1950s, when the scheme was first drawn up, the Lion Yard area was used as a surface car park, and the idea was to build shops there and on land nearby. It was described as the biggest redevelopment project in England, and the bulldozers started work in 1972, flattening everything along the

Before – Lion Yard surface car park.

After – work begins on the new shopping development.

south side of Petty Cury, where many of the city's clothes shops are now. Petty Cury was pedestrianised, but other old streets vanished, such as Alexandra Street, which linked Petty Cury with Post Office Terrace. The Lion Yard car park was built by the end of that year, and it was followed by shops, offices, and the new Central Library. Princess Anne came to perform the official opening ceremony in 1975. The scheme helped to boost Cambridge's reputation as a regional shopping centre. In 1959, the city's first arcade had opened, Bradwells Court, and in 1969, the Co-op had built a big shops complex at the Beehive. The same year, the market square in Cambridge got the chance to offer shoppers a bit more. Until 1969, much of it had been used as a car park, with stalls ranged around its edges, but it was realised it would be better for shoppers and traders alike if the cars were moved. As well as bringing extra shops, Lion Yard provided alternative parking, as did Queen Anne Terrace car park, opened in 1971.

Despite these changes, traffic problems continued to grow. Between the end of the 1930s and the start of the 1950s, the number of cars and lorries in the city had doubled, and the inadequacies of Cambridge's narrow, medieval streets had truly been laid bare. Park Street multi-storey car park opened in 1963, but queues of cars soon built up. The traffic even put the city's river bridges under increasing strain. Magdalene Bridge started to sag, and buses and lorries were banned from crossing it in 1967. Victoria Bridge was also regularly jammed with traffic funnelling into Mitcham's corner. In 1967, the corner was re-designed minus its roundabout, leaving houses in the middle of a traffic island.

The planners reckoned the city needed another bridge, and in 1971, Elizabeth Way was opened, but it too was soon filled with cars, motorbikes and lorries. When Lion Yard opened, its extra car parking spaces were welcome – but the overall impact there as well was simply to attract more cars.

The market square in 1964, before the cars were moved.

Park Street car park opening in 1963.

Bus jam, 1965 – Cambridge's narrow streets were not suited to modern-day traffic.

It was in the 1970s, too, that Cambridge began to develop as a centre for high-tech industry. Many factors contributed to the phenomenal growth. There was the engineering excellence of companies like Marshall's, which in the late 1960s had designed the distinctive droopable nose and retractable visor of the world's most futuristic plane, Concorde. There was the genius of the university's engineers, men like Sir Charles Oatley, Cambridge University's professor of electrical engineering, who headed the team which invented the electron microscope. The new machine used electrons instead of light rays, giving it a power so immense that objects could be magnified to more than a million times their actual size. It made it possible for

Work on the nose section of Concorde under way at Marshall's.

Sir Charles Oatley.

University experts working on an early computer, Atlas.

experts to carry out detailed research into viruses, and to look at the fossilised remains of simple cells, which helped to establish when life on Earth began. There were discoveries by astronomers, such as the pinpointing of pulsars, or pulsating stars, by Cambridge's Anthony Hewish and Jocelyn Bell in 1968. Working at the Mullard Radio Astronomy Observatory, they showed that the new stars could be perfect 'physics laboratories', allowing cosmologists to study what happened to matter in extreme conditions. Their work would not have been possible without the telescope innovations invented by the then Astronomer Royal, Sir Martin Ryle, another Cambridge man. There were inventors like F.T. Bacon, who lived on the edge of the city at Little Shelford, and who designed the fuel cell for the Apollo 11 spacecraft which took part in the historic first landing on the Moon in 1969. And, of course, there was

Star-gazing – Cambridge's Astronomy Institute.

Cambridge's role in the development of computers. Cambridge University's computer staff published the first book on programming in 1951, and introduced magnetic tapes in 1952. In the 1960s, they teamed up with the Ferranti company to build an advanced computer called Titan, and in the 1970s, they were involved in projects like memory protection, and developing a computer-aided typesetting

Acorn – led the way in producing computers for schools.

Cambridge Science Park.

John Bradfield.

system for Cambridge University Press. The microprocessor appeared in 1971, with several thousand transistors on a single chip, and six years later, the first home computer, made by Apple, appeared on the market.

Cambridge became a magnet for companies like Acorn, whose Archimedes computer joined Apple as one of the most popular computers in schools. Dutch electronics giant Philips also moved to the city, taking over Pye. Then, in 1975, the Cambridge Science Park was opened, the first such facility in Britain. It was built on land once used as a testing area for tanks, and the prime mover was the land's owner, Trinity College, whose senior bursar Dr John Bradfield led the project. The idea was simple – to turn some of the scientific research being done at Cambridge University into practical applications. However, the Science Park became more than just a testbed for new technology. It became a scientific community, where like-minded companies could work together, swapping techniques and ideas. One of the early residents was Cambridge Consultants, which had begun life as a tiny firm set up by three graduates in 1960. It employed university whizzkids to come up with all sorts of high-tech gadgets, such as a valve cap that emitted a signal when tyre pressure was low, a miniature 15-speed gear box, and a mini amplifier that fitted into a cigarette packet.

Dr Gordon Oswald of Cambridge Consultants with one of the firm's inventions – a ground-based radar machine.

Other inventions since have included red light-emitting diodes for pocket calculators, a machine that monitors audience numbers for television ratings, a new type of package for microwave food – which opens automatically when the contents are cooked – and the round tea bag. The firm has also conjured more speculative creations, among them a space sail – a 250-metre diameter craft that in theory could travel from Earth to Mars on solar power alone.

The new Addenbrooke's Hospital.

Clive Sinclair.

Cambridge's reputation for electronic wizardry was boosted by people like businessman Clive Sinclair. Balding, bearded and bespectacled, he invented an early digital watch, and began the craze for pocket calculators. Then he came up with a mini TV, with a screen just two inches square, and went on to launch the first personal computer priced at less than £100.

The city's high-tech revolution won the approval of the first Prime Minister with a science degree, Margaret Thatcher. Visiting Cambridge in 1979, she declared: 'Cambridge is a goldmine. It is a place where the brains and talents of those in the university can be harnessed and developed by industry so that new products can be made and new jobs created. There is a wonderful interface between the academic side and the business side, and Cambridge is one of the prime areas in Britain where we can see this happening. It is a wonderful success story.'

At the same time as the city was building its international reputation for engineering science, its medical experts were enhancing its credentials as a health pioneer. The principal location for their work was Addenbrooke's Hospital, which in 1962 moved from the building it had occupied for two centuries, in Trumpington Street, to a big new site in the south of the city. The first phase of the new hospital, at the end of Hills Road, was opened by the Queen, and further stages of construction followed quickly. The Medical Research Council established labs there, and many of the top research specialists from around the country, and the world, came there to work.

One of the doctors who flourished in the new surroundings was Roy Calne, one of the great names in the field of transplantation. When he first came to Addenbrooke's in the late 1950s, his research had to be carried out in a cramped single room above a flat in Fitzwilliam Street, but by 1968, he was working at the new hospital site, and it was in that year that he carried out Europe's first liver transplant. A liver from a dead person was transplanted into a 46-year-old woman from Girton, near Cambridge. The patient later died, but Dr Calne, now Sir Roy Calne, was not discouraged. He and his team carried on with their work, and with the discovery of anti-rejection drugs like cyclosporin in the 1970s, their transplant success rate improved dramatically.

Another huge medical breakthrough was made by two Cambridge doctors in the 1970s. In 1969, Bob Edwards and B.D. Bavister, working with Oldham-based gynaecologist Patrick Steptoe, had begun experimenting with a technique to help women who desperately wanted a baby, but were unable to conceive. The technique was called in vitro fertilisation, and involved removing an egg from a woman, fertilising it in the laboratory, and then re-implanting it in the mother's womb to develop as a normal pregnancy. The three doctors carried out experiments on women volunteers for nearly a decade before trying it for real, and on July 26, 1978, they saw their dream come true. Louise Brown, weighing in at 5 lb 12 oz, was born – the world's first 'test-tube' baby.

Roy Calne.

Patrick Steptoe (left) and Bob Edwards talking about their pioneering work to journalists.

Soon after Louise's birth, it was revealed that Edwards and Steptoe were working on deep-freeze experiments. The idea was to freeze embryos so they could be implanted in the womb at just the right time in a woman's hormone cycle. They were also looking at helping infertile women by giving them fertilised eggs from other women. The deep-freeze idea opened up a science fiction-style possibility – children being born a century after their parents conceived them.

Just as incredible was the discovery of monoclonal antibodies in Cambridge in 1975, by Cesar Milstein. Commonly called 'magic bullets', they were specifically manufactured antibodies that could be used to attack unwanted cells such as cancers, and they opened up the

Cesar Milstein.

The Cambridge Rapist – Peter Cook, and the mask Cook used.

possibility not only of curing that disease one day, but also of creating 'designer' drugs that could tackle other illnesses as well.

One thing that the city did not want to be famous for in the 1970s was the terrifying presence of the man who came to be known as the Cambridge Rapist.

In June 1975, a heroic police officer wrestled a fleeing suspect to the ground near a student hostel at Newnham, where a young woman had been attacked. The man was Peter Cook, the Cambridge Rapist, and his arrest freed the city's women from eight months of fear. From October 1974, Cook, 47, a van driver from Hardwick, had carried out a string of attacks on women. Some had been raped, others violently assaulted. Police, with no clues as to who was responsible, had warned women to stay off the streets and lock their doors. On the day he was arrested, Cook had gone to the hostel in Newnham intent on raping a girl there. He had earmarked his victim, a Canadian-born medical clerk, with meticulous care, and entered her room silently, with a knife strapped to his chest.

When she saw him, she screamed, and he slashed at her, cutting her arms. Then he fled, pursued by several residents. A short while later, a policeman saw a man pedalling towards him on a bike, and when the cyclist refused to stop, he grappled with him. It was Cook, wearing a blond wig, and he was overpowered and taken away. When his home was searched, detectives found a variety of disguises, duplicate keys for hundreds of bedsits, and plans of their internal layouts – as well as a chilling list of potential victims. They also recovered the rapist's terrifying hood, made from a leather bag, with the word Rapist painted on it, and a zipper mouth, which when open gave the impression of shark's teeth. In court, Cook admitted six rapes, and a number of other assaults. He was jailed for life.

Cambridge United enjoyed its best-ever days in the 1970s. At the start of the decade, the club finally succeeded, after many years of trying, in winning election to the Football League. The achievement sparked joy in the city. At the time, the team was on a tour of Germany, where they had won three of their four matches, and when they arrived back in Britain, an army of fans was there to greet them. The team drove with them in a triumphant cavalcade to Cambridge, where they were greeted by thousands more people in the streets. Soon after joining the league, the

*Conquering heroes –
Cambridge United
players celebrate
winning Football
League status.*

club won promotion from the fourth to the third division. More than 10,000 fans, a club record, packed the Abbey to see United clinch it with a 3-2 win over Mansfield. Although they slipped back down again, they achieved the feat again in 1977, under the guidance of manager Ron Atkinson, becoming fourth division champions once more, and earning promotion to the third. The following season, they went even higher, into the second division.

There were changes to Cambridge's local councils in the mid-1970s, and to the city's schools. Local government reorganisation in 1974 got rid of the old Isle of Ely and Huntingdonshire districts, and created a new Cambridgeshire County Council, based in Cambridge, and two new district councils, East Cambridgeshire and South Cambridgeshire, the latter also based in Cambridge. In the late 1950s and early 1960s, two new secondary schools, Netherhall and Manor, had been built to meet the need created by post-war housing. Now, the city got its first Community College, Parkside, the city version of the Village Colleges, followed soon after by another, Coleridge. Cambridgeshire's two High Schools, the Boys and the Girls, became sixth form colleges – Long Road and Hills Road.

Cambridge University finished the 1970s on a note of change, too. The all-male colleges of King's, Churchill and Clare decided to admit women, there were big extensions to a number of university buildings, and a new block was built at Queens'. Homerton, a teacher training college, was brought into the university fold, and the Music School opened, in West Road. The university also got a new Chancellor – the Duke of Edinburgh.

It found one of its greatest ever benefactors too, the millionaire businessman David Robinson, who

David Robinson.

Robinson College.

lived locally. At this time, there was intense political pressure to increase student numbers, but most of Cambridge's colleges were already stretched to capacity. David Robinson stepped in with a huge donation – £20 million – to enable a brand new college to be built. Appropriately, it was named after him.

Modern Times

THE building of the Lion Yard shopping centre had transformed the middle of Cambridge in the mid-1970s, and in the mid-1980s, another big retail complex did the same to the city's Kite area.

The Grafton Centre had been talked about by the planners for three decades before it finally opened in 1984, and it was one of the most controversial shopping developments in the city's history. The Kite area was very rundown in parts, but residents did not want to see homes bulldozed to make way for shops, and they mounted a fierce campaign to stop it happening. They called themselves the Kite Community Action Group, and organised marches and fund-raising shows,

The Grafton Centre –
opened in 1984.

*Demonstration by
Kite residents.*

backed by celebrities like Clive James and Michael Palin. The battle led to planning blight, prompting businesses to shut up shop, including the well-known Laurie & McConnal store in Fitzroy Street, and in the end, in 1978, councillors reached agreement with Grosvenor Developments to go ahead with the new shopping centre, which was opened by the Queen.

The advent of the centre with its national chain stores like Debenhams and C&A, and the arrival of other retail giants in the historic city, was a factor in the demise of many of Cambridge's smaller shops at this time. Rents began to rise, and so did rates. Wards cycles and electrical goods, Bacon & Ora tobacconists, and specialists like Grays bookbinders in Green Street and Pigotts tools in Sussex Street, all closed, while Barrett's china shop moved out of the city. Bodger's the tailors – a city shop for nearly 140 years – Coad's drapers and tailors, and Gallyon's gun shop were other casualties. Cambridge had simply become too expensive for them to survive.

House prices were on the up and up too, stoked by the city's emergence as a prime location for the new high-technology industry. Traditional firms like Marshall's continued to prosper. In 1982, during the Falklands war, the company got a surge of work modifying RAF Hercules planes for mid-air refuelling, and it has since opened a plush new car sales centre. But dozens of new, smaller

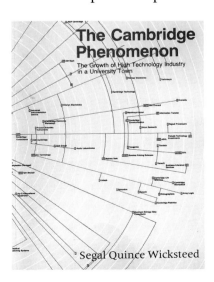

*The Cambridge
Phenomenon report.*

businesses were being attracted to Cambridge as well, specialising in computer software, medicine, and other emerging areas of research. In 1985, a detailed analysis of how this was changing the city was published – the Cambridge Phenomenon report. Written by business consultant Dr Nick Segal, of Segal Quince Wicksteed, it charted the rise of the electronics firms from the 1970s through to the 1980s, and revealed how they were clustering together so they could feed off each other and exchange ideas. At the time the report came out, Cambridge had more than 260 such businesses, employing 13,700 people. One of the biggest was Acorn, which had 400 staff, and a turnover of £90 million.

The report urged the planners to help the phenomenon grow, by providing better leisure amenities and better shopping, and it acted as a blueprint for other towns and cities around the world too. Dr Segal's dream was that one day, Cambridge would be the high-tech capital of Europe – and today, the city can rightly lay claim to that title.

Big flop – Sinclair's C5.

The Cambridge Science Park now has more than 60 companies on it, and the nearby St John's Innovation Centre, which opened in 1988, has more than 50. Many smaller, computer-orientated firms have got started in the villages surrounding the city.

Not all the ideas dreamed up in Cambridge in the 1980s made it big, of course. One of the most spectacular flops was Clive Sinclair's C5, a battery and pedal-powered tricycle with a range of 20 miles. It cost £399, but it never captured the public's imagination as an alternative to the car or the motorcycle. Only about 14,000 were ever made. At the end of the 1980s, Sinclair, by then Sir Clive, sold his Madingley Road home and moved to London, and in 1990, his Cambridge Computer firm quit the city and switched to Scotland. Undeterred by the C5 fiasco, he went on to bring out two more high-tech bikes. In 1992, there was the Zike, a little electric bike light enough to be picked up with one hand, and two years later came the Zeta, the Zero-Emission Transport Accessory, an electronic box that could turn a normal cycle into an electric bike.

Weather forecaster – Joe Farman.

The university's reputation for science was further enhanced in the 1980s. Three of its top researchers won Nobel Prizes – Fred Sanger in 1980, for his work on DNA, Aaron Klug in 1982, for discoveries in molecular biology, and Cesar Milstein in 1985, for developing his method of producing monoclonal antibodies. For Sanger, it was a unique double – his second Nobel Prize, making him the only person ever to win the Chemistry prize twice.

A team of experts at the Cambridge-based British Antarctic Survey, led by Joe Farman, made another earth-shattering discovery in 1984 – that there was a hole in the ozone layer above the Antarctic. The stratospheric layer helps to protect the Earth from the harmful effects of the Sun's ultra-violet rays, which can cause skin cancer and eye cataracts, kill plankton, and damage crops. Man-made chemicals like the chlorofluorocarbons used in aerosols, released into the atmosphere, were responsible for breaking down the ozone, Farman said. Combined with the release of other substances, such as lead,

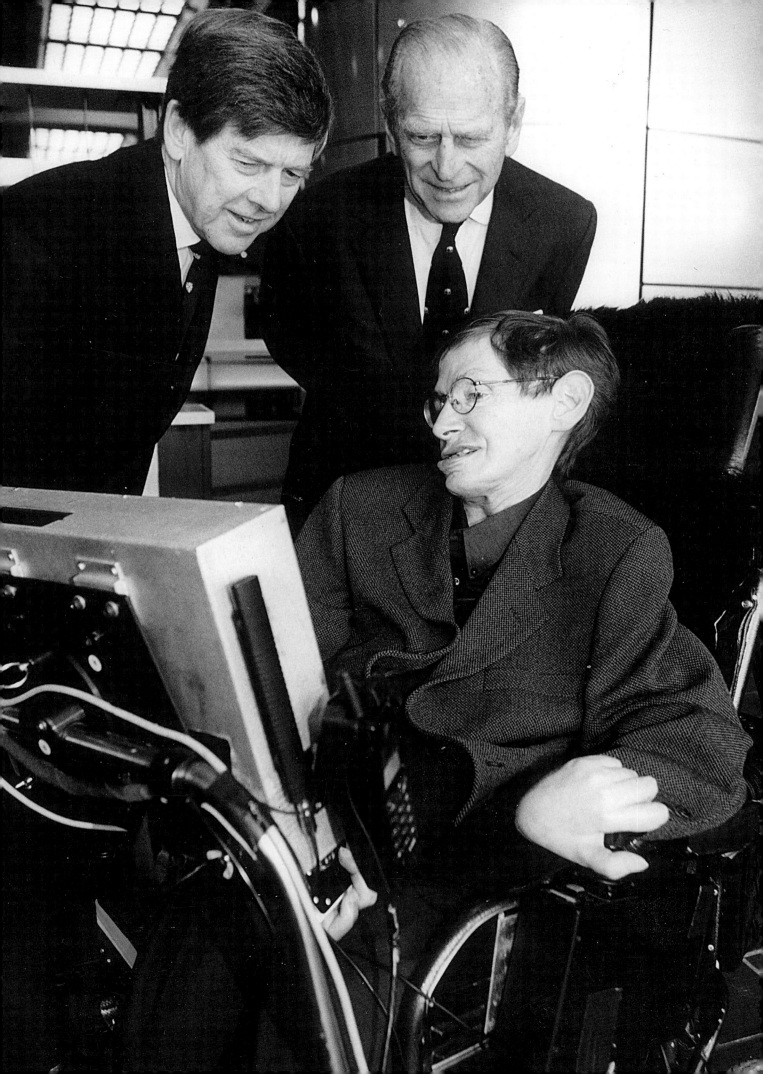

benzene, nitrous oxide and carbon dioxide from car exhausts, it was causing global warming. The planet was slowly but surely getting hotter – the so-called Greenhouse Effect – and it could lead, the scientists warned, to increasingly frequent storms and rising sea levels, which might swamp areas like East Anglia. The International Institute for Applied Systems even created an image of Cambridge-on-Sea – with a 23 ft rise in sea levels turning the city into a coastal town by the end of the first third of the 21st century.

Another university scientist worried about the future of the planet was the man who has become the world's first science mega-star, Stephen Hawking.

Born in Oxford in 1942, he studied physics at University College there, and then moved to Cambridge to do research in cosmology – the study of the universe.

He switched from the Institute of Astronomy to the Department of Applied Mathematics and Theoretical Physics, and became Lucasian Professor there in 1979 – the chair previously held by Sir Isaac Newton. The event which brought him into the public spotlight was the publication of his book *A Brief History of Time*. It came out in 1988, and explored his theories of the universe, including phenomena like Black Holes. By 1996, it had become one of the biggest selling books of all time, with eight million copies sold.

Hawking's scientific genius was given added poignancy by his disability – he suffers from amyotrophic lateral sclerosis, which affects the motor skills. Confined to a wheelchair, he can only speak by touching a computer screen, which is connected to an electronic voice. His voice has been used on pop records and TV ads, and in 1998, the then-US President Bill Clinton asked to meet him at the White House to hear his ideas on what the world of the future would be like. Prof Hawking told him it was likely to be peopled by genetically-engineered human beings. He has since delivered an even more cataclysmic message – that the Earth could be heading for its own destruction.

Cambridge University got a royal student once again in 1983, Prince Edward. He came up to Jesus College, starting off on a degree course in archaeology and anthropology, but later switching to history. The young prince's academic work was far from his main interest, however. His passion was for the stage, and he got involved in Cambridge University Light Entertainment Society, student Rag, and Cambridge Youth Theatre, taking part in several productions. In 1991, the prince personally backed a £300,000 cash appeal for the theatre group after its council grant aid was cut.

The following year, former Pembroke College man and Cambridge schoolteacher Ted Hughes succeeded Sir John Betjeman as Poet Laureate. Hughes, a Yorkshire-born grammar school boy, had met and married fellow poet Sylvia Plath in Cambridge in the 1950s. She was a student at Newnham College, and while she completed her studies at the college, Hughes took a teaching job at Coleridge School. The couple later moved to London, and tragically, Plath took her own life there, gassing herself in their flat.

Cambridge University dons joined forces with students and residents at the end of 1988 to fight a threat to the university's Veterinary School. A Government-commissioned report said the country had too many vets, and two schools should shut down, Cambridge and Glasgow. Academics and students in Cambridge were

Prof Stephen Hawking, with Cambridge University's Vice-Chancellor Sir Alec Broers, and the Chancellor, Prince Philip.

*Royal wrestler Prince
Edward taking part in
a Cambridge drama
production in 1987.*

stunned. The Vet School was a leading light in the field of animal health – the first trials of many anaesthetics, now used widely in veterinary practice, had been carried out in the city. A protest campaign was mounted, the issue was raised in both the House of Commons and the House of Lords, and a petition with 200,000 names on it was delivered to 10 Downing Street. The following year, a review revealed the original report had got its sums wrong, and that more vets would be needed in future years. The Vet School won a reprieve.

The Rosie Maternity Hospital.

Among the new facilities for human health was the Rosie Maternity Hospital, born in 1983. Opened by the Queen, it cost £6 million, and replaced the old Victorian hospital in Mill Road, no longer up to coping with the needs of the city's growing population. Half the cost of building the new hospital came from TV

rental tycoon David Robinson, the man who had already donated the money to establish Robinson College. Although the Rosie was finished ahead of schedule, its opening was delayed by contamination in its piped medical gas system. Then two months after it did open, one of its wards had to be closed due to a shortage of nurses.

A couple of years earlier, people in the Cambridge area raised £1 million to give Addenbrooke's Hospital one of the finest pieces of medical equipment in the country, a state-of-the-art body scanner. The efforts of the appeal's main organisers, John and Kathy Phillips, earned them a letter of congratulations from the Prime Minister, Mrs Thatcher, in which she praised their 'magnificent achievement.'

The hospital also saw an unexpected but welcome influx of public money in 1984 for its liver transplant programme, thanks to a little boy called Ben Hardwick. When he was just a toddler, the two-year-old from Surrey, who needed a transplant, appeared on Esther Rantzen's *That's Life* programme to highlight the desperate need for organ donors. After the TV show, viewers sent in £110,000 in donations, which was used to set up an intensive care unit at Addenbrooke's, and the programme helped to find an organ donor so Ben could have a transplant. The story sparked a big row over the funding of transplantation, and led to a big increase in the number of operations carried out – because more people were

Brave Ben Hardwick, with father Billy and mother Debbie.

carrying donor cards. Tragically, however, brave Ben died a few months later. He had to have a second transplant – and even though surgeons led by Professor Roy Calne battled through the night, they could not save his life.

Saving children's lives was the spur for two of the country's greatest-ever athletes to go head to head in Cambridge in 1988. Sebastian Coe and Steve Cram, watched

Sebastian Coe beats Steve Cram in the Great Court Run, 1988.

by millions of TV viewers around the world, re-staged the Great Court Run at Trinity College, the athletic ritual made famous by Lord Burghley, and immortalised in the film *Chariots of Fire*. They raced against each other around the college quadrangle, in a bid to beat the 46-second record set by Burghley in 1927.

Coe was the winner – and he beat the record too, clipping 0.48 seconds off it. The race, which traditionally had to be completed within the time it took the college's 400-year-old clock to strike noon, was all about raising money for charity. The two runners took on the challenge to collect donations for Great Ormond Street children's hospital in London.

All smiles – Princess Diana at Cherry Hinton in 1989.

The Princess of Wales, Princess Diana, came to Cambridge in 1989, for what was one of the most popular royal visits ever. She visited a project for former alcoholics in Cambridge, and then went to Milton, to open the new Children's Hospice, a special hospital for terminally-ill children. She was visibly moved by the plight of the children, and delighted to meet local people who had worked so hard fund-raising to get the project started. Later in the day, she opened a new £700,000 village centre at Cherry Hinton, then the biggest of its kind in the Cambridge area. The three-hour visit, eight years before the Princess's tragic death, epitomised her appeal to ordinary people. Looking stunning in a red two-piece suit, she was all smiles, chatting amiably to the crowds who had turned out to see her. Many of them had begun gathering several hours before she arrived, eager to get the best vantage point.

Despite the large number of young people living there, Cambridge had never had much to offer them in the way of entertainment venues, until the mid-1980s. There were a few nightclubs, but the only venue for concerts in the city centre was the Guildhall, which was limited because of the size of its halls. Frustrated by the lack of a place to dance, drink and listen to music, teenagers started staging illegal

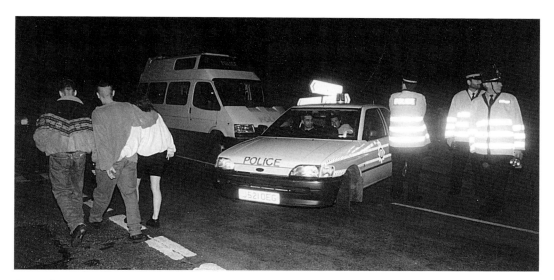

'raves' in disused buildings, including a former cycle shop, an old pub in Cambridge, and a disused building in nearby Girton. Clashes with police were the result, and councillors held a meeting with 100 young people to resolve the crisis. The upshot was the formation of the Cambridge Venue Group, which pinpointed a site on the old Cattle Market in Cambridge where a meeting place-cum concert hall could be built. The move was supported by the city's mayor, John Woodhouse, and by Radio 1 DJ John Peel, and the city council came up with the money needed. The new building, called The Junction, opened in 1990 – the UK's first purpose-built youth venue. It has gone on from strength to strength, and in 1999, it won a £5 million grant from the National Lottery to fund major expansion plans.

At about the same time as The Junction came on the scene, music lovers got another decent-sized venue. The city's former Corn Exchange was revamped and re-opened as a concert hall.

The late 1980s and early 1990s saw more changes for the university. In 1989, the Cambridge Foundation was launched, a body which set itself the task of raising £250 million in 10 years, mainly from business sponsorship, to fund the university's research plans. The following year, multi-millionaire businessman Paul Judge, former boss of Premier Brands at Histon, near Cambridge, gave the university £8 million to found the Judge Institute of Management Studies, on the site of the old Addenbrooke's Hospital. The idea was to turn out better managers for Britain's companies, and the scheme was backed by other businesses, including Barclays, Peat Marwick, and Guinness, which pumped in £1.5 million to fund a professorship.

The city also became one of the world's leading centres for astronomy, when the Royal Greenwich Observatory was re-located in the city, although it was only a brief stay. The 250-year-old observatory, the western world's oldest scientific institution, moved to Cambridge from Sussex in 1990, but in the years that followed, it was subjected to several lengthy reviews, was threatened with privatisation, and experts even suggested that it should be run by a consortium of universities. Finally, in 1997, the Government body in charge of funding pure science, the Particle Physics and Astronomy Research Council, recommended the RGO should close to save money, with some of its work being switched elsewhere. There was a fierce campaign in Cambridge to keep it going, which won support

from famous astronomers like Patrick Moore – but the closure went ahead in 1998.

The Royal Greenwich Observatory was not Cambridge's only connection with the stars in the 1990s. The Hubble orbiting space telescope, meant to open up many of the mysteries of the universe when it was launched, was partly designed by Cambridge scientists, although they may later have wished they had no link with the £3 billion eye in the sky. It was dogged by technical problems, suffering everything from blown fuses and bent solar panels to blurred vision. However, it later sent thousands of spectacular pictures back to Earth, among them images of rings of glowing gas encircling an exploding star 169,000 light years away. It also recorded a cataclysmic event in the solar system – the Shoemaker-Levy 9 comet ploughing into Jupiter.

In 1995, Professor Sir Martin Rees, Plumian Professor of Astronomy and Experimental Philosophy, followed in the footsteps of many of his predecessors in Cambridge, and was appointed Astronomer Royal. The same year, a young man whose parents lived near Cambridge, Michael Foale, was picked by NASA to be the first Briton to walk in space. Aerospace company Marshall's was also aiming for the stars, converting a Lockheed TriStar to launch rockets and satellites into space.

Other big developments for the university were the arrival of the Royal Commonwealth Library in the city in 1994, and at about the same time, the completion of the Granta Backbone, a system of online computer links which used a network of fibre optic cables running under the city's medieval streets. It allowed the university to become one of the first institutions in Britain to start regularly using the Internet. The Isaac Newton Institute for Mathematical Sciences opened in Clarkson Road in

Previous page: Building work under way at the Corn Exchange.

Far-sighted – campaigners trying to stop the closure of the Royal Greenwich Observatory in Cambridge.

Left: Astronaut Michael Foale chats to the mayor, Joye Rosenstiel, during a visit to Cambridge.

Far left: Prof Sir Martin Rees.

The Law Faculty.

1992, and in 1995, one of the most spectacular buildings anywhere in Europe, the Law Faculty, was completed, a vast, ship-like structure designed by Sir Norman Foster.

Cambridge got a second university too. Anglia Polytechnic was granted university status in 1992, in line with Government policies to expand higher education by a third. The new university, based not only in Cambridge but also on campuses in Chelmsford and Colchester, immediately announced plans to double

the field, sat down, and then darted off at speed. The animal in his video film, later enhanced by computer experts, was identified by a Cambridge University zoologist as either a puma, jaguar or leopard. There have been other sightings of the phantom beast since, notably in 1996, when children at St John's College school were kept indoors after reports it was lurking in the school grounds. However, no one has ever come close to capturing the animal.

Cambridge tried had to solve its biggest modern-day problem, traffic, in the 1980s and 1990s. Some of the schemes were effective to a degree – but others were a total flop. One relatively successful idea was pedestrianisation, which was introduced in several city centre streets, including Sidney Street, where cycles were banned during certain hours of the day. The move made little impression on many of the foreign students who flood into the city for language courses every year. They regularly flouted the ban there, and in other streets. However, it was popular with many shoppers, who felt it made the city centre more 'user-friendly'. Also popular were measures to improve facilities for cyclists. An enormous network of cycle routes was established, including a giant cycle bridge near the railway station, the longest of its type in Western Europe.

The least popular scheme was Tow-Away, introduced in 1992. Illegally parked vehicles were clamped and hoisted onto the back of a lorry, then taken to a pound at Clifton Road, where their owners could reclaim them. The fee to have a vehicle released was £95, and those who failed to reclaim their car within 24 hours were

Anti-car: pedestrianisation was one solution to Cambridge's traffic problems.

Off you go – cars that were towed away cost their owners £95 to reclaim.

charged £12 a day storage. Some drivers of older cars reckoned it was not worth shelling out – and simply left their vehicles sitting at the pound. There was considerable anger about the inconvenience of it, too. Single women complained that they had been stranded at night after their cars were towed away. A charity worker answering an SOS call came back to find his car gone. War veterans attending Remembrance services found their vehicles had vanished – even the Mayor's car was hauled off. One Christmas Eve, Tow-Away crews impounded the cars of 40 last-minute shoppers. After three or four years, illegal parking had been cut dramatically, but at that point the scheme became uneconomical. With fewer cars to tow away, the company carrying out the operation decided it was no longer profitable, and it was shelved.

The biggest flop was the Green Bike idea. In a bid to persuade people to use cycles instead of cars, city councillors obtained hundreds of old cycles, had them repaired and painted green by young offenders, and left them at bike parks around the city.

Residents were invited to hop aboard free of charge, pedal to their destination, and then leave the bike at a bike park for the next user. At first, it looked like a winner. All over the city, community-minded citizens were seen pedalling from place to place. But after a few days, reality clicked in – and nearly all the bikes went missing.

Some later turned up in strange places, such as under park benches, and in the River Cam, but most never came back. Leading councillor Simon Sedgwick-Jell said at the time: 'It was the victim of human nature. It only needed 100 people out of Cambridge's 100,000 population to foul it up.'

What does the 21st century have in store for Cambridge?

The city lost one of its big annual events, Cambridge Festival, in 1992, due to spiralling costs, but it has since seen improvements in leisure facilities, many of them funded by the National Lottery. In 1995, the lottery gave Cambridge Arts

The Warner Bros cinema complex.

Parkside Pool – revamped thanks to the National Lottery and the city council.

Theatre a £6.4 million grant so it could be refurbished, and the same year, Warner Bros opened a multiplex cinema in the Grafton Centre, which was also expanded with more shops. Cambridge's ageing Parkside Pool, built in the 1960s, was demolished and re-opened in 1999, again with lottery backing. More amenities are on the way, with plans to develop the city's old Cattle Market, which closed after holding its last fatstock show in 1991. Another cinema and a bowling alley have been proposed there. Cambridge United has also announced a scheme to revamp its Newmarket Road stadium, providing more seats. The club reached the quarter finals of the FA Cup in two successive seasons, in 1990 and 1991.

The city lost two of its best-known stores in the 1990s. The Joshua Taylor department store, a century old, shut down in 1992, and in 1999, Eaden Lilley closed, although it has maintained other shops in and around the city. The other big department store, Robert Sayle, part of the John Lewis Partnership, looked set to follow suit at one stage. The shop, which dated back to 1840, had outgrown its St Andrew's Street premises, and was looking for another site, possibly on the outskirts of Cambridge. In 1997, however, the Shearer property group came up with plans to revamp the city centre's shops, in a scheme called Grand Arcade. It proposed building a new, bigger Robert Sayle store as part of the development, and lots of smaller shops as well, up to 50 of them, together with restaurants and cafes. In addition to the city centre scheme, there are plans to further extend the Grafton Centre.

As the city grows, so does Cambridge University. It began developing a big new complex in the west of the city in the late 1990s, providing more science buildings, among them a new computer laboratory, and the UK headquarters for computer giant Microsoft. The development was announced in 1997 by the university's Vice-Chancellor Sir Alec Broers, and Microsoft's Bill Gates, who revealed he had given the university a gift of £12 million towards the cost of its new lab. The university also intends to develop a swathe of land it owns in the north-west of the city, building houses for its staff, and possibly making room for a brand new

Cambridge college. There are about 15,000 students in Cambridge, and numbers are expected to keep on growing rapidly. By 2009, when the university celebrates its 800th anniversary, there could be 2,000 more.

Today, Cambridge is regarded as the top centre in Europe for high-tech research and development. It is leading the way in developing the Internet. Local firms were among the first to offer connection to the World Wide Web, and to develop interactive television. Cambridge was the second city in the UK, behind London, to create an Internet cafe, and MP Anne Campbell has helped to set up Online Cambridge, a scheme to give people access to computers in public places. In 1999, the Government announced the city would be the host for a £3 million national Entrepreneurship Centre, aimed at fostering new business talent. There are now more than 1,250 high-tech firms based in and around Cambridge, employing 32,000 people. The companies are involved in biotechnology, telecommunications, such as mobile phone and Internet innovations, medical research, and a wide range of other disciplines.

However, as the city celebrates its own Octocentenary, it is facing perhaps the biggest challenge in its history. Its spectacular economic success has made it the fastest-growing area in the UK. People are flocking to Cambridge to work – and there is a desperate need for more new homes, and for more space for new companies to get started.

Bill Gates, with Vice-Chancellor Sir Alec Broers, seated, announcing the collaboration between Cambridge University and Microsoft in 1997.

The Grafton Centre – further expansion is planned.

Cambridge celebrating its Octocentenary in January 2001.

Super-village – Cambourne.

Sightseers – Cambridge will remain a magnet for visitors.

Two years ago, work began on the biggest new settlement in Britain, Cambourne, a 'super-village' seven miles west of the city. When complete, it will have more than 3,300 houses, two schools, a church, shops, a hotel, sports facilities, and a business park. It will not, however, be big enough to meet the demand for housing. The planners have been considering allowing another big community to be built near Cambridge, with Army land at Oakington and Waterbeach the favourite sites, each earmarked for tens of thousands of homes. The city council is also investigating the idea of extending the city to the east, building houses on what is now Cambridge Airport, and on land near it. Marshall's, which owns the airport, has offered to relocate if it can find a suitable site elsewhere.

The A14 – choked with cars and lorries.

Putting up more houses will mean encroaching on the Cambridge Green Belt, the ring of land around the city that has been largely a no-go area for building since 1965. It will also create a need for major improvements to the city's infrastructure – building more facilities like schools and hospitals, and roads. Local councillors have drawn up the Cambridgeshire Transport Plan, aimed at coaxing drivers out of their cars and onto buses and bicycles, but roads like the A14, once filled only with marching Roman legions, are now so choked with cars and lorries that they urgently need widening.

While all these questions are resolved, there is one certainty: Cambridge's rich heritage and scenic splendour will continue to make it one of the most admired, and most visited, cities in Europe. Every year, more than three million tourists make the pilgrimage to see the river, the colleges, and the surrounding countryside – and as the 21st century begins, Cambridge is sure to remain a magnet for millions more in the future.

Index